Love, War, and Other White Lies

A Poetic Diary of Love, War and Other Topics

By

Tony Bethel

1stBooks – rev. 09/08/03

white lie – a lie concerning a trivial matter, often one
told to spare someone's feelings.

Source: Webster's New World Dictionary Third
College Edition

About the title:
It is my opinion that love and war have many
similarities. The passion in which we love may be
compared to the passion in which we fight. The effort
we give to individuals may be compared to the effort
put forth in individual battles. The small lies we tell to
put us in good favor with a potential lover may be
compared to the small twists in truth that our own
government gives in relation to political issues. May
God always bless America and may America bless the
world with her goodness. It is my belief that freedom
of speech and expression are the true tests of a free
society. In my writing I am given the privilege to
express those rights.

MY DIARY

OF LOVE

AND OTHER

TOPICS

"Love, War and other white lies, don't be
surprised if you refuse to open your eyes."
                                        -Tony Bethel

10-04-98

Love Is A Verb
(For all women)

I wonder why you won't say how you feel. Then it
became apparent that although it is unsaid, it is not
unheard; because your actions show love is a verb. I
wonder why I don't hear those eloquent words used by
you to express how you feel about me, now I realize it
is the things you do that I must see. Although love is
unsaid it is still heard because I know for you love is a
verb. Pretty words strung together may sound nice, but
they cannot combat the world which at times is as cold
as ice. I understand now, like taking a healing herb
that love is not just a thought, love is a verb. Many
poets write long and hard searching for the word or
phrase that fits just right; whether it is complex or
simply trite. Although it is left unsaid I have already
heard, for I now realize that love is a verb.

Come Grow With Me
(For Carolyn)

When I am with you I feel immense, much like a
Redwood tree, please come—come grow with me.
When I have you by my side I am filled with such joy
and pride, limitless—like the vast open sky. When I
touch you I now understand the creation of the
universe because I feel the passion of the explosions,
twisting and turning, the powerful forces and desire to
release what is in me into you and become one with
creation. Come grow with me for I am a youth
expanding in your presence. I am rediscovering things
I have forgotten. You reawaken in me things which
were dead and now I grow and grow and grow. Come
grow with me, let us expand together mentally,
physically emotionally, spiritually. Let me reach
inside you and you into me until we touch upon the
very soul of the other and hold it in our hands and feel
its warmth and the glory of God's pure love. Come
grow with me and we will joyfully chase many
tomorrows, leaving behind yesterday's sorrows. We
will go forward, savoring each day together as a
starving man savors a good meal. Come grow with me
and we will unlock the mysteries of this planet, just
you and I. What works for me could work for you if
the effort is renewed. With every meeting my feelings
are replenished like a mountain stream, and how
refreshing you are. You allow me to grow and grow
and grow. Come grow with me.

10-06-98

Mother
(For Ruwanda)

Though you were not like most mothers you are still
my mother, and even though time and space; life and
death separate our realities
I still came from you—I still acknowledge you.
Youth can be such a bitter time, full of memories,
some
bitter as lime.
What I wanted most you were unable to give.
What I needed most strangers fulfilled.
How can this be when you are my family…So I
thought
So many thoughts in such a young mind, twisting and
turning all the time. Wanting the stability of a family
life, somehow replaced with unstable strife.
Others provide what you should give, yet as I grow I
can
forgive—not for your sake, but for my own.
To make these memories grow still with time and
make
sense of this life and how you fit in it.
My mother by birth, yet not my friend.
Time will resolve such painful wounds.
But who will I cling to when they finally do.

10-07-98

My Twin
(For Jane and Janet)

In the womb I felt your heart beat next to mine, so
close, so warm; now many years later though the miles
separate us, I still feel you close to me. Although our
lives have taken different paths, I still feel bound to
you like steel, yet loose as a feather because I choose
to be bound to you. Where you go, I go, though I may
not be there physically, I am there in spirit—where
ultimately all things go. I remember the times of
trouble where we held each other tight. I remember
the moments of joy where the laughter lasted forever.
Still bound, one sound of loyalty, of trust, of devotion.
Where you go, I go, though I may not be there
physically, I am there in spirit—where ultimately all
things go. In our day to day lives, we have taken
different paths yet we cross from time to time and at
the crossroads, we recount the joys and the sorrows;
the triumphs and defeats, still bound, one sound of
love, of commitment, of emotion. Who knows how
long a thread the fates have given us to spend, yet we
enjoy each inch, each strand as though it were our last.
Although we hope that one may not pass before the
other, we are left with the memory
In the womb…

7

10-8-98

Paint Me A Picture
(For Dee)

Paint me a picture of words with bright, vibrant colors
speaking of joy and laughter. Paint me a picture of
words that remind me of a warm, sunny day in the
park. Paint me a picture of words which make me
reflect like a pond, in the deep green woods. Paint me
a picture of words where I can see the blue calm of the
ocean and feel the refreshing white coolness of the
waves. Paint me a picture of words, where I can see
the change of the seasons with the changing colors of
the leaves from a bright green, to faded green, to
yellow, to red, to orange-tan and then brown.

Paint me a picture of words of these moments with
you, to capture my joy and happiness and all the good
that you bring to my life. Paint me a picture of words
that express the ecstasy I feel when I am with you.
Paint me a picture of words that reflect the warmth of
your touch and heat of my passion.

Paint me a picture to see that we are just a speck of
dust in a vast universe, yet that speck of dust is a
universe unto itself. Paint me a picture of words where
there are no colors but the colors of imagination, and
where seeing is not done by the eyes, but by the spirit.
Be my third eye to the world beyond this. Unlock
those doors which are closed from my understanding.
Paint me a picture but use no paint—let your words be

9

like paint on the canvas of my mind and therefore the picture will exist throughout time and I will carry it with me always, until I die.

Black Athena, Queen of Sheba
(For Janet)

Oh how I am impressed by you, the way Solomon was
of the African queen. You are so beautiful yet
intelligent—a thinking man's dream. I long to be with
you and you may call me a dreamer, but you are my
Black Athena, Queen of Sheba.

I now know how the ancient Greeks felt in awe of their
Gods and Goddesses. When I see your perfectly
chiseled features and delicate frame, yet wise
countenance; I can only think of my favorite Goddess
and I become the dreamer, because you are my Black
Athena, Queen of Sheba.

You are the woman spoken of in proverbs who is the
strength of her man, yet stands alone. The one who
nurtures and is the source of nourishment. Oh how my
mind is satisfied by your wisdom and soothed by your
presence. My eyes are satisfied by your slim and
graceful figure. I know I am a dreamer, but you are my
Black Athena, Queen of Sheba.

When I think of you I think of perfection personified.
It was you who Plato was speaking about when he
mentioned the "perfect forms." Your beauty is
timeless, eternal, everlasting. You refresh my soul as a
cool breeze on a warm summer's day. How fortunate
for Solomon to know such beauty, wisdom, and grace;

11

coupled with spirituality and faith. Will I ever have you? Maybe? I am a dreamer! You are by Black Athena, Queen of Sheba.

10-10-98

In The Quiet Of The Night
(For Danah)

In the quiet of the night, crickets chirp and fireflies
beam radiant for affection, they dot the darkness like a
thousand small stars. In the quiet of the night I hear
the symphony of silence and enjoy it like a night at the
opera. In the quiet of the night I feel your warmth
radiate and envelop me even though I only hold your
hand. In the quiet of the night I absorb your presence
the way a dry old sponge absorbs water. In the quiet of
the night the darkness surrounds us like a thick cloak
so warm, so cozy. In the quiet of the night the soft
music of the radio translates the romance that is in my
heart for you. In the quiet of the night I long to be with
you wrapped so tight like one warm swirl of passion.
In the night I long to feel your heartbeat next to mine
and I count the beats of love's clock and feel its
rhythmic intensity escalate. In the quiet of the night
where few words are spoken volumes of thought and
feeling flow between us with the directness of a laser
beam. In the quiet of the night as I kiss your cheek, I
am aware of the possibility of what could be, yet I am
faced with the reality of the moment and satisfied to be
with you, in the quiet of the night.

10-12-98

Betrayal
(For Connie & Nancy)

Tell me how does it feel to have the knife so deep in
my back and why do you still twist it so, can you not
tell I am already dead? What gain is there for you
when I gave my heart so free, yet you spurned me and
enjoyed it. What sadistic glee can you gain from
hurting me now? Weren't my cries enough? Wasn't
the pleading enough? Weren't my sacrifices enough?
Now I am left with nothing. What now do I have to
give to another lover? Yet this you did on purpose.
You want to disable me, you want every man's face I
see to be you. You want every man's touch to be your
touch. You want that I should live in this constant
prison with your ghost as the jailer. You want to
emotionally imprison me. You are judge, jury, and
executioner. How could I have given so much and got
so little in return? Why was I not aware of the moth's
tragic burn that flew too close to the flame,
mesmerized by it yet destroyed by it. How ironic, you
are not around, yet my pain echoes your name and it is
the only name I hear, and you are not even around to
gloat in your victory. The ultimate humiliation, the
ultimate betrayal.

10-12-98

There Are No Mistakes In Love
(For Melissa)

I hate Cupid. Curse the Dove. There are no mistakes
in love. The highest emotion we could ever have
should be greeted with a smile and a laugh. Don't be
angry at things in the past; because how do you repair
a broke glass—you don't, you move on. There are no
mistakes in love and much like hand and glove love
goes with life and life with love. Don't be afraid, take
my hand for you are a woman and I am a man. So
simple a concept yet so hard to convey that love may
be lost in the simplest of ways. As we fell off our bikes
or fell off the horse we got back up and tried again, of
course. Though the broken heart is hard to heal unless
love is given it never will. Only in having the courage
to give do we get the reward of the spoils; and to
appreciate love at some point we must toil. Yes, what
a task, what a feat no one said it would be easy. Yet
the reward is warm and sweet. There are no mistakes
in love because that is God's most precious gift from
above. You may not be able to see it, you may not be
able to taste it, yet when we cheerfully give to another
it is never wasted.

10-16-98

You Have Nothing To Offer
(For Janet)

You tell me that you have nothing to offer and that I should wait. I tell you, you have given plenty and I want you for my date. You tell me you are empty from the lovers of the past. I tell you, you fulfill me and they I will surpass. You tell me you are too busy and do not have enough time. I tell you, you fill my heart and that is very fine. You tell me others hurt you and scarred your giving heart. I tell you I would not be here if it weren't for your gentle heart. You tell me I have to wait until it is right. I tell you as long as it takes I will keep you in my sight. You tell me you are hurting and have no time for love. I tell you let me heal you, let me be your love. You tell me it won't work and things will repeat. I tell you, your presence in my life is such a welcome treat. You say you have nothing to offer, yet you have already given so much: your thoughts, your feelings, your kiss, your touch, and I appreciate it all so very much. What you have given I need. What you need I can provide, just stand with me by my side. Be my beacon in the darkness. Be my lighthouse on the shore. Guide me into your safe harbor. Envelope me with your love. Give my ship a home no longer bouncing up on the waves but safe in your calm harbor. You have more to offer than you will ever know. Let me examine your magnificent gifts one by one, until my sail meets the setting sun.

10-17-98

The Face Behind The Mask
(For Dee)

I want to see the face behind the mask. I want to know
it and caress it, love it, and protect it. Although the
mask is for protection it also serves as rejection,
keeping strangers at bay to wonder—what is she
thinking today? Let me in behind the mask the secrets
shared will be mine alone not to be revealed but to be
felt, cherished, then sealed within my heart where they
will be safe from harm. Show the little girl to me. I
will not hurt her or cause her harm. I only want to
entertain her and feel her charm. I see the little girl in
the twinkle of your eye and know she is just a
heartbeat away between a breath and a sigh. Let her
come out to play because she is amongst friends
forever and a day. I know it is hard to let go, especially
when you have been injured so. Just trust me once to
show you she is safe with me because I have seen her
before. I get so close then she runs away. I am then left
with hope for another day. What is this face behind the
mask? Are you afraid I will not like what I see? Just
understand that, that which is a part of you I want to be
a part of me. To absorb it, to horde it, to value it, and
to love it. Let your little girl play with my little boy
and we can share such wondrous toys of love, of
laughter, of this world and hereafter. Give to me and I
to you. Let us drop our masks and see the truth.

10-18-98

Come Visit Me
(For Janet)

Here I stand before you naked in spirit with my arms
open wide—come to me. I am open and waiting for
you to step inside—come to me. Welcome to my
world, my thoughts, my emotions, my love for you, my
strong devotion. Welcome, welcome to me. I achieve
balance with your presence, it is you who calms the
fires that burn within me. It is you who beckons me to
start again, to finish the unfinished, to live the unlived,
to do the undone—to be, come visit me. Open the
door and step inside, feel the cool breeze hit you in the
face, that is me. Refreshing, yet stimulating. Relaxing,
yet invigorating. Miles and miles of space open and
free. Miles of vastness, miles of me.

Come, I wait to embrace you, to touch you, to hold
you, to encompass you, to wrap you in my love.
Welcome, welcome to me. Come as you are with no
falsehood or pretense, no offence or defense. Come as
you are I will accept who I see. Come step inside.
Come visit me.

10-18-98

My Visit To Olympus
(For Janet)

I visited Olympus today and sat amongst the Gods. I saw things there that mere mortals only dream about. I conversed with a goddess and was held spellbound by her beauty. I sat upon her couch and enjoyed the comfort mere mortals could not begin to understand. I saw volumes of literature and I was so surprised, because if Gods knew everything what reason would they have to read, but I guess even Gods need entertainment. I read to a goddess one of my poems. She smiled her radiant smile and I could feel her strength through her clothes and I was filled with such earthly desire for this queen of the universe. I visioned her firmness pressed against my body. I am entertained by the music of the muses and my head spins in ecstasy. I have made it to Olympus and like the gates of heaven being opened for the first time I am excited and giddy as a little child. I see a wondrous lake from Olympus and the view is relaxing and placid like my beautiful goddess. I feel like yelling to the world this triumph, yet I am as meek as a lamb. I visited Mt. Olympus today. I held a goddess in my arms. I am a mere mortal and lived to tell my tale, how blessed am I.

10-18-98

The Ice Has Broken
(For Carolyn)

I felt the ice break today, you trusted me with
something valuable, you. You invited me to a place
that few people have ever seen but once they are there
it is a place they rather not leave. I feel the warmth
melt the ice and I realize something I already knew, the
beautiful niceness deep inside of you. As the thick
icicles fall away, I feel the newness of spring come this
day. Winter is waning, I increasingly see the sun in
your eyes. This is a sure sign that spring has just
begun. Beneath the cold crisp air lies the seeds of life.
Beneath the tender, warm earth waiting to be
awakened by the heaven's gentle rain are those fertile
seeds; like the sleeping eggs in a woman's womb
waiting to be awakened by the rush of sperm. Life!
Life! Life! All will be awakened, but first it is the ice
that must be broken.

10-20-98

You Are In Me
(For Deirdra)

When I hug you ever so tight I absorb your essence—
you are in me. When I hold your hand, stroking it,
caressing it, fondling it, kissing it, I feel your touch—
you are in me. When I kiss your cheek, the time seems
to linger as I try to enhance this moment and elongate
its duration, so you will be in me. I feel you in me
every time we meet. With every greeting, I feel you in
me, warming me, holding me, lifting me, challenging
me. You take my mind to another level. With your
inspiration comes words of elation which I translate
into a poem. It is in me where your spirit has a home
and there are so many rooms, and yet you fill every
one of them. I am full, full of life, full of you. It is as if
I have tapped a new energy source and that source is
you. Vibrant, electric, magnetic, shocking,
stimulating—you. You are the battery that gets me
through this endless day and fills my lonely night. You
are in me!

10-25-98

The Storm Within
(For Jane E.)

I have a storm within. Can't you feel my heart crash
against my chest the way the waves crash against the
rocks? Can't you see the dark clouds in my eyes that
appear out of the blue like a hurricane? Can't you hear
the thunder in my voice when I call your name? You
stir me so; my deepest passions are like a cyclone
hitting a small island. I feel the restlessness in my
loins. Can't you feel the lightning between us, the
electricity, the power? I feel the force of a tornado
when I am around you. I want to whirl you about in
my arms and carry you off in the wind to make love to
you in my private cloud, to release the floodgates of
nature and burst through the dam. Can you feel it?
Can you feel the water rise with the downpour from
the sky? Can you feel the forces of nature in me? I am
hot like a forest fire for you, consuming all within my
path; how I would love to consume and sear your flesh
with infinite passion. Can you feel the heat, the red hot
heat of desire? I want to run deep inside you; the way
a meteor does when it hits the earth. It is so fierce and
direct inside the earth, burning and twisting as I want
to be in you, natural and free. Like father sky and
mother earth and how her parched soil welcomes his
warm moisture. It is no wonder she is so fertile and
blooms with pride as she blossoms in full womanhood
from the developing seed. This world was created
with one cosmic storm of violent gases and lightning

and crashes; sparks flying in the darkness as lovers wildly embrace in the night letting seething love spill into the darkness, creating light, creating life. Can you feel the storm within?

10-26-98

God's Blessings
(For Dee)

When I think of the perfect warmth on a sunny day
when the children are out to play, I think of God's
blessings. When I think of mom's homemade apple
pie steaming on the windowsill and the fresh smell of
juicy apples, I think of God's blessings. When I think
of the way of a man with a girl and her beautiful
silhouette outlined by the sun, I think of God's
blessings. When I think of the jobs I have had and the
money I have made and lost, and the strength God has
given me to face another day, I think of God's
blessings. When I think of the second coming and the
uncertainty of this earthly life I do not fear but I think
of God's blessings and how He has allowed me to
come this far. When I think of the triumphs and the
failures, the pain and the joy all of these things that
make up life and life is God's blessing. When I think
of a man and a woman coming together to create a new
life, I know it is with God's blessing. God's blessings
are as simple as a sunset and yet as complex as the
Gordian Knot. God's blessings are as beautiful as the
plumage of a proud peacock, yet if misused they could
be as fatal as a cobra. God's blessings are with us
every day; we must have the courage and common
sense to realize them.

11-14-98

I Missed Something
(For Janet)

Somewhere along the way I missed something you
were trying to say. All finger pointing aside, I care for
you deeply, and that I cannot hide. The poems I write
to honor you so that you may know my feelings are
true. Yes, I have acted upon impulse and although
certain things were discussed, it is the perception
which confused us. You saw one thing and I another.
Although your words were clear, it was my ears which
were not working properly to pick up the message sent.
Sometimes you must tell a fool twice for him to hear
the first time. It is not that the fool's hearing is a
problem, only his understanding. So make the fool
understand, so his ears will be open. Although I may
have missed something that does not make the
situation hopeless or the subject clueless. I strive to
understand so that I may see. Today I missed
something but you have made it clear, I now move
with confidence, instead of fear.

11-27-98

It Does Not Come
(For Jane E.)

I hold my pen but the words do not come; like trying to pump a dry well; this is the feeling all writers will live to tell. That emptiness in the head where all words seem dead, where inspiration is lax and where writing is slack. I can't seem to put it together. I have encountered my creative stormy weather, now I am in the blues and the grays and I wonder if the words will come today. Such a vast emptiness, such a long pause, and I wonder if I have forgotten the cause. Why is there such emptiness, why don't the words come out, I feel God has struck me blind, deaf, and dumb. Why can't I pick up where I left off. My thoughts just wander and I scoff at the idea of having another idea to write about. Could this be the end, the last poem to write. I don't think so, not tonight. For as long as I can think and write on what I think, there is hope, and with hope comes the promise, and with the promise comes the action. Although the thoughts do not come now, they will—somehow.

11-27-98

Sleep
(For Carolyn)

The nighttime mother holds me close in her embrace
and I rest my head upon her chest. My weary soul
clings to her, enjoying the comfort she has to offer. I
stare into her dreamy eyes and I am under her spell. I
am intoxicated with her, she lulls me and I feel
comfort, I feel at rest. I feel safe with my head upon
her breast. I want you, I want to be with you and stay
forever, but you only give me a few fleeting hours and
like a drifting lover you are off again. You tell me so
many stories in the night and they all dwell within my
head. Some stories are peaceful, some fill me with
dread; yet they both dwell within my head and are
played night after night like movies at a picture show.
As I lie upon your silky bed with my head upon your
breast, I am pleased, ever so pleased that you come to
give me rest.

11-27-98

Dining With My Goddess
(For Janet)

I went to Mt. Olympus today and dined with my
Goddess. She prepared a meal with her own two
hands. She works her magic in her kitchen, and I watch
in amazement, in awe, in patience of receiving the
delicious meal made. The smell of the food tugs at my
nostrils and I am taken prisoner. I will go where you
want. Your preparation is so effortless, you are like a
sorceress working a magic spell and I am under your
influence. You drive me mad with your calm, stoic
countenance; yet you exude the maximum desire with
your ageless beauty and your sensual movements. I did
not realize how sexy cooking could be. I help with the
preparations as a hopeful lover who wants to advance
his cause, yet you keep going without a pause to the
next step, the next phase, by now I am in a daze. Is it
the Chardonnay or is it your graceful ways that have
me intoxicated? I sit here by your feet ready to eat the
meal we prepared. I realize I am in Olympus with my
goddess dining on a gourmet meal; I ask myself how
much better can it get. I have the answer, it doesn't.
So I enjoy the moment, I enjoy you.

11-28-98

I Thank You Lord
(For Janet)

I thank the Lord for our first meeting, of your radiant smile, of your pleasant greeting. I thank the Lord for our summer apart, it was a good test of what was in my heart and my feelings for you. Lord is she the one? Let my dreams come true. I thank the Lord for our second meeting, still a radiant smile and a pleasant greeting, a sweet peck on the cheek, a flower to give, my knees felt slightly weak. I thank the Lord for things we have in common like movies, theater, music, art, tennis, church and dining. Things that are plain and refined. I thank the Lord for such a beautiful face and eyes that follow you from place to place. So expressive are your expressions, so deep your thoughts. Such power and strength, yet so feminine and vulnerable. You are a lady full of class. I lift up my glass and toast to you, thank the Lord, for my dreams have now come true.

11-28-98

The Embrace
(For Diane)

When it is performed correctly it is all the contact you
need; such warmth, such caring, such beauty, such
sharing. At times more intimate than intercourse, at
other times more casual than social discourse.
Sometimes it may leave you empty wanting for more.
At other times it is more satisfying than the finest gold.
I want to hold onto you forever; to savor your flavor,
your presence, your smell, your essence. The embrace
is the Alpha and the Omega. It is what we give upon
meeting and departing and whatever occurs in
between. It is the embrace that serves as a screen
dividing the platonic from erotic and which path do we
choose? Should we go for ease or go for truth. It is the
embrace that magnetizes me to you. I feel your
strength in it. I detect your passion in it. It is the
embrace I use as a tool to take me to a higher place,
and that place is you.

10-30-98

Loneliness
(For Carolyn)

Although your time away is temporary, I feel the void your absence has left me. I long to be with you and go to the places we enjoyed together. The simple joys of life seem so empty. My food has lost its flavor. My drink has gone flat, and my soaring heart has plummeted. Please explain this black hole in my life, where all thoughts center around you. Your beautiful image haunts my mind like a vivid specter of the past. What a seductress you are to have stolen my heart for ransom, and I await your return so that I may have it back. Each day seems like an eternity. Each hour is like a slow painful death. How I long for your touch; like the dry grass yearning for rain during a drought. You replenish my whole being. You are the nectar to my soul. Come back to me so that I may sip upon you and bask in your radiant presence and be fulfilled by your eternal love. Your love is so powerful and bright like the sun and is the source of my inspiration. Just as the clouds obscure the light and deprive the earth of her love, the sun. I feel spurned by your absence. How I await your life giving embrace, I wish to absorb you so you can be with me always. I wish to be one with you; not just for physical pleasure, because that is limited to the earth. I also want to connect on the spiritual level, so our bodies are conduits of the great spirit and we feel the power of creation when we love. Although I am lonely now I know soon I will not be alone and the two shall become one flesh and my loneliness will be no more.

10-31-98

When Titans Fall
(For President Clinton)

When titans fall what a loud crash they make, with reverberations that ring throughout the world. What a loud thud that is made and how many are hurt from the debris of the fall. How many people suffer from the repercussions? How could a man's error run so deep and be so far reaching? When great men fall it is as if one of the Gods fell out of the sky and landed here on Earth...with the rest of us mortals. Here we are examining this God, realizing they are not too much different from ourselves. Why do we put such people on those high pedestals only to have them plummet from the sky; to crash to their death here on Earth as Icarus did when he flew too close to the sun. His sin was not flying too high, but his sin was forgetting that he was human. We are all human, with vices, whether it be of thought, of the flesh, or food, or drink, or drug, or intolerance of those who are less than perfect. When titans fall, we all feel the loud thunderous crash as if we were in an earthquake. As man created the Gods, so we choose to believe and put our trust in others. If our trust is unfounded, then we must face the error in our decision and the reality of man being a man...nothing more nor anything less.

10-31-98

I Pursue
(For Janet)

The way a buck pursues a doe, I pursue you. The way
a stallion pursues a mare, I pursue you. The way a boy
pursues a girl, I pursue you. With the intensity and the
single minded purpose to be with you. Not just in a
physical sense, but in all senses. In the physical. In
the intellectual. In the emotional. In the spiritual. In
all senses, I strive to be with you. To be one with you.
To know your love and have you know me for who I
am, and who I strive to be as I strive to know you for
who you are and who you strive to be. I pursue you as
a challenge yet as a reward for all my past failings. I
pursue you in the hopes of making a better tomorrow
not only in my life but in our lives as one. As I strive
for this goal I want us to be together to pursue each
other and each other's interests; to cherish the presence
of the other. I pursue you to know your mind, to know
your spirit, to know your feelings, to know your body.
To be in you in all aspects of life. It is all aspects of
you that I pursue, the more you share with me the more
I can give back to you. So I pursue. I pursue. I pursue.

10-31-98

Precious
(For Carolyn)

More precious to me than gold, you shine so. Valuable
you are, so bright, like a diamond's brilliance. Your
kindness and wisdom radiates through that beautiful
smile of yours. You are as sturdy and steady as silver;
valuable, yet practical. I long to touch your beautiful
dark skin like the smooth, cool onyx stone, your dark
eyes warm me like heated coals on a cold winter's
night. Pragmatic yet beautiful, elegant yet reachable,
you are my earthly star, my guardian angel. You are so
pretty, yet you do not seek adoration, but give it. You
do not absorb light but it bursts forth from you like a
flower of the sun showing your warmth to all that get
close to you. You are so precious to me, more than
you will ever know. You give not of things but of the
spirit. Your internal light inspires me and gives me the
energy to accomplish, the will to keep going, and the
desire to win. You are more valuable than platinum,
and I hope our relationship is as strong and vibrant as
that precious metal.

10-31-98

When Faith Is Lost
(For Dee)

What happened to Santa Claus, The Tooth Fairy, Guardian Angels, and the God of Sunday school? The all encompassing, omnipotent, all powerful, unquestioning faith of a child. Where did all of these images go and when do we lose our faith, become cynical, and turn into another face in the crowd, another dandelion amongst the weeds. When do we settle on the chains of mediocrity instead of fighting to be free? When do we lose our faith and why? What makes us stop believing in God? When is our faith shaken as Peter's was when he walked upon the water and sank when he lost faith. We too sink when we lose our way. When we say we are too big for God. When we say we are too smart for God. When we say we are too rich for God. When we say we are too powerful for God. When our faith fails, so do we. We become as ships in the night, navigating to the shore after losing the beacon of guidance. We have lost the stars of the night to steer by. We take God for granted like the stars in the night that He will always be there, but what if all the stars were gone? What a great darkness that would be, and if God were out of our lives, what a great darkness of the soul. We may be able to live without the light of the stars, but we cannot live without God's spiritual light, for as the Earth would wind down to die without the sun, we too die when our faith dies.

10-31-98

And So I Write...
(For Janet)

I cannot fight all of the racists of this world—and so I
write to displace the anger.
I cannot love all of the women in the world—and so I
write to capture the beauty of their faces, as well as
their souls.
I cannot have all the money in the world and so I write
of splendor, of grandeur, of opulence and of the
romantic elegance I desire.
I cannot have all of the power in the world—and so I
write with strength, passion and energy. I write
convincingly and poetically to move you to your very
being.
I cannot have all of the knowledge in the world—and
so I write to give my view of this planet and our
universe and my interpretation of it. I write to give my
experiences so others will not fall into the abyss I am
now leaving. I write so others will not make the
monstrous errors that will devour their lives as they
have devoured my wretched existence. I cannot have
all of the pleasures of this world—and so I write of the
sensual and erotic, of the sensuous and the sexual. I
write of the imagination and the physical manifestation
of that imagination.
I write of the glory of the dance, the expression of the
desire, and its execution and consummation. I write of
the passion, and the body's surrender to that passion as
two bodies, two persons, become one and how in the

beautiful mystery of God the blessing of life from the ultimate union of man and woman is manifested. As man was from woman to be born; man must be in woman to create—and what a beautiful canvas a woman has. A beautiful landscape of many colors and moods all waiting for the artist's touch to give and receive. And so I write, I write, I write of the glory in the day and the passion in the night, I write, I write, I write.

I cannot see God's magnificent, glorious face—and so I write of the majesty, and the power, and omnipotence that is God's alone. I write of the questions I ask in doubt and of the answers God has given in his infinite mercy. How wondrous is your love. How powerful are your miracles. You have saved me from myself and protect me from my enemies. You alone have given my soul an everlasting oasis from the desert of sin and desperation. Your love is so great I cannot fathom it. I can only write of your countenance of your beauty, of your great Son. One day I will be free from this earthly shell of a body and then I will be free to see, but for now I write, I write, I write giving praise to my God during the radiant day and into the tranquil darkness of the night.

Passion
(For Janet)

A kiss ignites the flame, and the flame burns within me
and I want it in you. Passion has hit me like a lead
weight dead in my heart without hesitation. The fire
from that peck on the cheek ripped a hole in my heart
and made my knees weak. A series of kisses follow
like several brush fires. I embrace you as if my life
depended on it. I hold you as if to absorb your very
essence. I reach out to you to quench this fire in me.
Give me your mercy, set me free. I lay my head upon
your chest and I feel the warm softness of what I want
to caress. I am in ecstasy and in misery. Torn between
the peaks and the valleys, I want to travel it all. To
climb the peaks and venture the canyon. To have my
ship navigate your stormy sea and set course into your
beautiful fjord. I can feel the waves rise. I can feel the
storm swell, and I wonder am I between heaven and
hell. I want to ride your rapids and taste your
mountain stream. I want to know your mountains and
have you live in my dreams. I want our commitment to
be as eternal as the rocks, yet show no sign of aging.
Like the smooth pebbles that are constantly renewed at
the river's edge by the moist remembrances, it is the
refreshing memories of the past that keep them looking
new, though they were born eons ago. I feel the
passion and I fight it. I feel the waves crash at me like
the rocks on the beach and like the rocks I stand firm,
slowly eroding wave after wave. It is like when I touch

you. I am a little weaker than before. You consume me and you are my favorite obsession, my one true passion.

11-07-98

I Am Not Him
(For Roby)

The one that hurt you—I am not him.
The one that did those awful things to you—I am not him.
The one that did not commit to you—I am not him.
The one that broke all of those promises—I am not him.
The one that broke your heart—I am not him.
The one that used you—I am not him.
The one that abused you—I am not him.
The one that left you—I am not him.
The one you lost interest in—I am not him.
The one who refused to make you happy—I am not him.
I am not him, but I am me. Give me a chance to make you happy. Give me a chance to set your soul free. Give me a chance to dance with your soul. Give me a chance to put the twinkle in your eye. Give me a chance to put that lift in your step. Give me a chance to put that sway in your hips. Give me but one chance. That is all I need. That is all I deserve. Give me one chance to show you—I am not him.

A Poem A Day For Janet Lynn

A poem a day for Janet Lynn. A poem for my lover,
my mentor, my friend. A poem of poems for a queen
of queens. You are the lyric to my melody. You are
the glove that fits my hand. You are the woman for
this man. You are the one who completes my soul.
You turn my half into a whole. So many things I could
say about you; all of them beautiful, all of them true. I
follow you with my eyes, and the eyes do not lie. I see
the window of your soul. You have opened up to me
and I feel a gust of you as powerful as a hurricane, as
gentle as a lamb. You are the special woman for this
difficult man. Difficult because I want a real woman,
not one that just sits on a page. I want a lively woman
with passion and a dash of rage. I also want a duchess
and a diplomat—you are all of that, and more. Here I
stand knocking at your door. Open up and let me
inside. Say you will be mine and fill me with pride.
Mine, in the sense of my obsession. Nowhere near a
physical possession. I don't think any man could own
you. But I know others have unsuccessfully tried; and I
know for a fact you injured their pride. This is one
poem in the day of Janet Lynn, a beautiful person, a
wonderful friend, a deep warm woman who is in
constant search for a better tomorrow. What does the
day hold for us today. I grab your hand and we are on
our way, for every day with you is an adventure.
Every day with you is a mystery unfolding. Every day
with you is a blessing from God. Every day with you

63

hope springs eternal and love is renewed. Let me into your wondrous life to share your nights and plan our tomorrows. Let me commit to you and the poem will never end. The poem of Janet Lynn, my lover, my mentor, my friend.

11-08-98

In The Hands
(For Janet)

The way I touch you, the way I make you feel, it is in
the hands. The way I hold you and the warmth there
for you, it is in the hands. The way I feel your smooth
honey brown skin and the desire to be within, it is in
the hands. The way I embrace you and you embrace
me, it is electric, and psychedelic, like a different
dimension in a different place and time; it is not just in
your mind. There is no plan, it is all in the hands. It is
in the hands the way I make you feel. It is in the hands
of softness, in the hands of steel. Touching your body
gives me the energy I need. It is your body that
invigorates me. It is through touch that I am free. It is
in the hands that I translate the love for a woman from
a man. I feel what words cannot convey. My touch is
in your memory, forever and a day. It is in the spirit of
love that I touch your body, yet your body is love in all
its sweetness, in all of its kindness, in all of its warmth,
in all of its desire. My touch for you burns eternal in
your mind and in your heart. I feel your warmth touch
my heart. When I touch you I feel the real you—what
is underneath, what is true. What you try to hide and
don't want others to know, my hands feel your body's
secrets and keep them safe from harm.

11-08-98

Don't Stop
(For Nancy)

When I put my hands upon you, your body says don't stop. When my finger tips explore your curves and softness, don't stop. When I feel your roundness and your firmness, don't stop. When I touch your hills and slide into your valley, don't stop. When I feel the wetness of your sweet river, don't stop. When I unfold your beautiful rose, petal by petal, kissing it, stroking it, tasting the dew left by nature's ecstasy, don't stop. How I envy the bees the way they roll into the flowers as I would love to roll into you, nonstop. I feel the joyful beat of your heart when I am with you, don't stop. I feel the softness of your cheek and I kiss it to taste you, to know your taste and remember it so that I can savor the memory of it and of you, don't stop. I embrace you to hold onto your very being, to absorb as much of you as I can, to be into you as a man and, don't stop. To bridge the gap of the real and the fantasy. The slow roll which builds to the climactic release, don't stop. Don't stop. Don't stop!

11-09-98

Mother Earth
(For Janet)

Mother Earth how sexy you are. I want to taste the sweet berries on your firm round hills and roll them in my mouth and have them tickle my tongue. Then I want to run down your smooth plain to the lush curly grass of your valley. I want to feel the moist dew upon your grass left by your interlude with father sky. I want to course your rapids and drink from your eternal spring. I want to travel in your love cavern with my boat to enjoy the beautiful adventure of you. Mother Earth you are so beautiful. I want to put my plow into your dark moist fertile soil and sow the seeds of life. Mother Earth you are so sensual, the way the trees sway back and forth, tempted by their lover the wind. He makes their branches wave, reaching out to embrace him, but he teases them by changing direction, constantly whirling and twirling them about as if in an erotic invisible dance that we can only imagine. Mother Earth how pleasing you are. You bear forth tasty succulent fruit to be savored by the senses. You have given us the animals to learn by their sensual example, as when the stallion chases the mare tirelessly until she submits willingly to the pleasurable mount. Mother Earth, you have given us so much, yet we greedy humans have given back so little. Don't stop loving us, you are our mother, don't abandon your errant children. We love you. We need you.

11-09-98

The Chicago Wind
(For Jane E.)

The Chicago wind whips and cuts like a knife, much
like the city's pain and strife. The Chicago wind lifts
and carries much like our own hearts are lifted and
carried on a warm sunny day. The Chicago wind can
be cold and unforgiving, like a spurned lover who
ceases to care about living and only wants to destroy
all in its path. The Chicago wind can sway and tease,
the same way a beautiful woman can bring a man to
his knees. The Chicago wind can swoop down like a
hawk on high and attack its prey with the blink of an
eye; relentlessly, unmercifully, painfully—God please
help me. The Chicago wind can take you by surprise
and have you curse and fear the sky. The Chicago
wind whistles in the trees with powerful gusts that
have you begging, please. The Chicago wind is most
cruel in the winter when it is at its cruelest and most
bitter. The wind in the spring is a little more sweeter
with the coming of fertile life and beautiful creatures.
The wind of the summer blows hot and steamy, laden
with humidity. Some days we are lucky and a cool
breeze sneaks by. The wind of autumn I like the best of
all, the crisp way it catches our attention and makes us
stand straight, yet not so bitter as to make us hate. The
Chicago wind, enemy and friend; lover and foe, with
every passing day we Chicagoans never know. We can
only guess and hope the wind gives its best.

71

11-09-98

The Face
(For Janet)

I remember the face, the way her bangs curl teasingly upon her forehead, tempting me, challenging me to come closer. I remember the face with the twinkle in the eyes like a distant star leading north to freedom, guiding, loving, and protecting from harm. I remember the face with the cute chiseled nose that is so delicate and discerning, yet is never turned up at anyone. I remember the face, the beautiful, angelic chin that I long to touch, so delicate, yet strong; it adds wisdom to your expression. I remember the face and those beautiful lips that speak such eloquent words that I love to hear. I am charmed and beguiled by you. You have such beautiful lips I wonder about their taste. Are they honey, mint, cherry; whatever the taste it must be refreshing, uplifting, and inspiring. They take me to the highest heights, to the summit of this world, bordering on the next. I remember many things about you but the face will forever be in my mind. Like the lyric, like the melody, the face is in my memory, haunting me, bewitching me, enticing me.

11-10-98

Secrets
(For Danah)

The things you told me from the depths of your soul,
from the bottom of your heart you entrusted to me.
You have given me parts of you for safekeeping. You
gave the treasures and pain of your past. You have
shared with me the scars both internal and external,
and I wept inside. How I would love to kiss your scars
away both internal and external. How I would love to
go into your past and undo the hurts, right the wrongs,
and turn all the frowns into smiles. I know it is our
experiences that make us who we are, but why must
the process be so painful and why does the trauma stay
although the ugly days are gone. You have given me
your secrets and like precious jewels I hold them close
to my heart so others will not know I have them. Your
trust is one of the greatest gifts you have given me and
I will not betray you; because those pieces of you are
in me forever, and that makes me a part of you,
forever. Some things should not be said but
experienced. You do not have to tell, I feel you like
the heat of a raging fireplace across the room. I feel
you, your passion, your warmth, your desire, your
kindness. I feel it like I feel the heat from the intense
flames. Your secrets are my secrets, I hold them dear
as I hold my very life and would rather die than give
them away.

11-18-98

The Senses
(For Janet)

You heighten my senses. You electrify my soul. You
lift my weary spirit from the deepest of holes. Every
experience with you is electrifying and totally
satisfying. You feed my senses. My eyes are drunk
with your beauty and I long to taste you, to devour
your sweet body inch by inch, to know your flesh as if
it were my own. I long to touch your body all over. I
crave it—it is an addiction to me. Your soft smooth
honey brown skin. It felt so warm to rest my head upon
your bosom. Never have I felt so nurtured, never have
I felt so safe. For the first time I envied children and
the way they rest upon their mother's breast. Thank
you for feeding me, for satisfying my hunger, for
quenching my thirst, and giving my ears satisfaction
with intelligent conversation. I hold your hand and
feel its softness and warmth against my own hand, and
I close my eyes wondering what it would be like to
have you touch me all over with your warm, sensitive,
loving hands. The spices you put into our food do not
come close to your spiciness and beauty as a woman. I
taste you with my eyes and what a delicious flavor you
are. Delectable and lovable. I hear your voice which is
clear, calm, and refreshing like a beautiful pond in the
woods. When I touch you, I feel the smoothness, the
femininity, the softness, the woman in you. You
satisfy me, all of my senses. Come with me so I can
feel the ecstacy.

11-19-98

Electric
(For Rosy, Sheila and Visionary Women)

When I look into your eyes, I see the spark. You are
electric. When I hear your voice, the melodic waves
enter my brain and I respond—electric. When I see
your face, I am drawn to you. I can't help it, there is
nothing to protect me, you are totally electric. When
we embrace I don't want to let go. I feel your power,
your energy, the strength. You energize me and I
cannot let go, like being shocked by a live wire. I
cannot let you go. I want to go further. I want to go to
the source of the power; to the core of the generator. I
want to feel it; the ultimate charge, the great
transformer. Let me in, let me experience you in
totality. Would I die if you did? I don't know. I don't
care. Don't try to protect it, give me your essence. It is
totally electric.

11-19-98

The Dance
(For Sara)

Don't say too much but tell me something.
Don't hold me too long, but let me embrace you.
Don't kiss me there, but let me kiss you.
Don't touch me there, but let me touch you.
Don't make love to me now, but let me talk about it.
Don't arouse me too much, but be interesting.
Don't be cold, but show me tenderness.
Don't turn me on, but show me you desire me.
Don't try to possess me, but show me that you want
me.
Don't be pushy, but be decisive.
Don't be too aggressive, but show me you are a man.
Don't be too sensitive, but show me that you care.
Relationships are a dance. You have to take a chance.
Some days it's a samba, others waltz. It could be a
conga, tango or maybe fandango.
What about a rumba or mambo. It could be as simple
as
a jig or as complex as a jitterbug.
So many people, so many dances. Come make me
happy.
Come dance with me.
Be my partner and we will go through the dance of life
cheek to cheek, month by month, week to week. Give
me
this dance, it is you that I seek.

11-19-98

The Voices Of Angels
(For Ruwanda)

With clarity and power and love, I hear the voices of angels. The herald of God's message from above, I hear the voices of angels. With intensity, driving, and lifting as a plane taking off, I feel the lift of my soul leaving this earth and heading towards the clouds. How triumphant I feel, how strong. I feel invincible, untouchable. I feel as though I have wings and yet I stand before you, planted firmly on this planet. The angels' voices tickle my ears and give me the inspiration to go on, not in spite, but in love. The angels help me and protect my body not to come to harm. Oh Lord, thank you for blessing me and lifting me to higher heights. With each note I take a step towards heaven, with each word my mind is in religious ecstasy. I fear not death, because your beauty is hidden from me and I want to reach you. I want to touch you. It seems that death would be a small price to enter your brilliant kingdom. I will wait and enjoy this life you have given me and the ability to enjoy this choir and their voices; sweet voices, loving voices, powerful voices, angelic voices. The voices of angels. The instrument of God.

11-19-98

Unlock Your Heart
(For Jane E.)

There it sits in a safe all alone and underneath ten
inches of cold hard steel in that metal box. Unlock
your heart. Others have tried to access it, but the code
is all wrong and they leave frustrated and angry instead
of trying patience. Your heart is locked not because
you don't care; it is that way because you do care. You
want the right love, the right fit. The right moment.
The right guy. You want all that, and is that too much
to ask? No, it is not, with such a valuable heart as
yours. Like a twenty-four carat gem it is brilliant and
beautiful, and precious; all the things that men desire
and strive for. They don't know how to access it and
you cannot tell them. Because how would you know
the difference between a thief and a saint. A taker or a
giver. You don't know, so you wait for the man with
the code, the guy with the key. The man that will set
your precious heart free. Am I that guy? Only heaven
knows, but until that time, I will try to crack the code.
Unlock your heart and set it free. Let me be the one,
give it to me.

1/19/98

Moments
(For Janet)

Life is a series of moments passing one to the next.
Sometimes quiet and uneventful; at other times with
great passion and power. These moments we are
blessed or cursed with because no one asks to be here,
we just are, we examine the images of our environment
and if those images please us we stay, if those images
don't please us, hopefully we may leave. Moment
upon moment, like wave upon wave wearing down the
rocks, our lives too are worn down by individual
moments each upon the other. Brick upon brick the
structure of our lives is made. Some of us are blessed
with fantastic structures to the envy of others. The rest
of us make due with average and the poor and the
wretched end up with shacks.
These moments are dealt out much like a dealer
dealing cards or a gambler shooting dice. Who knows
how the moments will accumulate in this life. Will
they be positive or negative. Will there be twists and
turns for the better? Who knows; and what about that
final moment, that last instant when the collection of
previous images and past moments flash before our
eyes before the end when we reach our destination, the
transition point. I say transition because the soul does
not die it just slips from one body to the next like a
magnificent actor changing from costume to costume.
The soul is constant. It is the costume—the body, that
constantly changes. In these collection of moments

87

and remembrances of images I will remember you from this life to the next. And although this relationship may not last it is the moment that I seek, that I crave, that I will hold on to.

11-19-98

Things Shared
(For Janet)

An exquisite breakfast; wholesome, sweet, filling and delicious—like you. A beautiful concert with angelic voices bombarding our bodies with power, with love, with warmth. A powerful sermon of truth, and honesty, of God's love for us and my love for you. A visit to a book store to expand our minds, to expand our consciousness, to expand our relationship, to experience each other. A trip to a diner filled with scrumptious smells, southern cooking, and southern hospitality. Around us are various knick-knacks of the past; things southern, down home, that we both identify with, that we recognize. Things we feel comfortable with, things shared. I remember the sweet, sticky, nutty pecan pie with ice cream, our two spoons dig in and share this pie, this moment, this is life— things shared. A walk, a joke, your laughter, a held hand, smooth jazz, a romantic drive, these things are common and simple, but they mean more, so much more when they are shared.

11-22-98

The Sensuous Cook
(For Janet)

I like the way your hands drift deftly over the
vegetables; so nonchalant and effortless. Your hands
are so delicate, yet purposeful and knowledgeable.
The hands move with such grace and beauty as they
prepare the food; chopping it, dividing it, placing it
with accuracy, energy and love. How fortunate I am to
observe you while you cook. To see you bend, to see
you sway, I could watch you cook all day. A gourmet
of food, a gourmet of love. I must be blessed from
heaven above to have such a sweet angel like you
prepare us such a sumptuous feast. I want to interrupt
you, to reach out and touch you, but then the moment
would be lost and what would it cost in such a valuable
friendship that we have. I spy upon your sweet
expression and the look of determination on your face
as you prepare our delectable plates. You please me
so, much more than you will ever know. Pleasure with
you goes beyond the body, it touches the very spirit
inside of me. All of this from cooking a meal. You are
so strong, with such great will, how sexy that is, my
soul you fill. I am so lucky today, for I have had a
good look at a beautiful woman, a sensuous cook.

11-22-98

Thanksgiving
(For Carolyn)

An invitation from a lover. A day shared.
Conversations unending. I am with you all day long
filled with happiness and feeling strong. What a day
we had today, filled with fun, food, and laughter. I am
so thankful for you, in the things you say and the
things you do. You know my feelings, and I feel for
you. I tell you that my feelings are true. Thanksgiving
is such a time to appreciate our rewards and the
beautiful things given by God. I am so fortunate to
have you now, to know your presence and love of God.
From church to the street, I carry your words with me
that are so sweet. I am thankful for you and what you
have to give. It is your small sacrifices that enable me
to live. You lift my soul and give it wings. Each day I
thank the Lord for bringing you into my life and to
make you happy is what I strive. Good food, good fun,
good film, good God—thank you.

11-27-98

I Dine On You

(For Janet)

Here I am in majestic surroundings enjoying the view;
I am dining, dining on you. I help prepare the meal,
looking at your slender frame. I adore your ways and
enjoy the view. I am dining, dining on you. We
discuss relationships, politics, entertainment, no
restraint. I enjoy your brain and how effortlessly you
think. I sit and enjoy the view. Yes I am dining,
dining on you. The meal is cooking, hot and steamy—
exactly how I feel when you are near me. I take
another sip of wine and I see how truly fine you are,
not just physical beauty but as a person too. I love your
view, so I dine, I dine on you. The meal is prepared,
more wine is poured; and I wonder what the future has
in store. I feel so close to you, close enough to taste, to
firmly hold your slender waist with all thoughts
focused on you, I dine, yes I dine, on you.

11-30-98

The Gathering
(For Carolyn)

They come from miles around, some by car, some by
plane, some by train. They come for the gathering.
They come wearing their best. They come wearing
their worst. Some will come blessed. Others will come
cursed; yet they come to the gathering. They come
with gifts others come to get. Some come just for the
hell of it; not knowing why, they just come to the
gathering. Some are loud and preachy, others come
quiet and meekly, both are related, both come to the
gathering. Some come bringing food, others come to
eat it; others just to sit and watch and bide their time.
They still come, come to the gathering. Some are
friends, some family some lovers, some haters, a
mixed bag of human beings. We all come to the
gathering, including me. Not knowing what to say, not
knowing how to act, we feel plastic until it is safe.
Then come the smiles, then comes the laughter, then
comes the shouts, the squealing, the enjoyment of each
other as sisters and brothers. We are all sitting, dining
happy and free. This is the gathering of friends, lovers,
and family.

12-02-98

Ebony Orchid
(For Cynthia)

So dark and soft are your petals, how I would love to touch them tenderly until I see nature's dew upon them. I would love to have my face in your flower to savor the sweet aroma and kiss the dew drenched petals. How I wish to be a bee so I could pollinate with thee. So fragile the flower, yet it stands firm through the wind and the rain, ever resilient to nature's ways. I want only to caress you, yet I would not dare pluck you, for that would sever your beautiful life. You would then be but a beautiful trophy, doomed to die without your source of life, your source of nourishment. I am content right now to watch your beauty from afar and wonder in my heart, what would it be like to be embraced by your petals, to taste your sweet nectar, to stroke your delicate stem. My ebony orchid how unique you are, how pretty you are. The other flowers view you with envy and see your natural sway in the breeze. So natural, so sensual you reach out to the sun for his warm love. You wait to be satisfied by the engorged clouds; to gently release the sweet life giving drops upon your open, swollen petals and how satisfied, you are after the rain. How sensual your beauty to see the silver droplets of life upon your ecstatic petals. Life comes full circle. I desire thee my ebony orchid how wondrous and beautiful you are and how fortunate I am to have you in my garden.

12-06-98

Endless Night
(For Terrie)

It started with sweet conversation, music to my ears. It could have ended with a concert that moved me to tears. In amazement the night was endless, as if frozen in time, but I don't mind for it seemed like an eternity since we last met, and I have missed you so much. Your glance, your touch, your embrace that I love so much. This night is beautiful to behold and embedded in my mind. The walk, the talk, the dinner, what a winner I am to have you by my side. Inside the theatre the beautiful sounds bounce off of us as well as bombard us; hitting and gliding, yet smooth, ever so smooth. I feel as if I could reach out and touch the music and experience each note like touching the finest crystal and experiencing the beautiful prism from the powerful sun. The night seems endless like the day is long, like your radiant smile, like your endless patience. After the concert there is so much more in store, like a long drive and a long talk; a lovely walk inside your mind, so precious is your internal beauty. You are a rare find like a precious metal, beautiful to behold, ageless, timeless, a beautiful star in this endless night.

12-06-98

Your Love Is Light
(For Antoinetta)

Your love is light and sweet like a chocolate mousse
and
it is so delicious to the soul.
Your love is light like the air on a clear night,
revealing
the brightness of the stars, and oh, how your love
shines.
Your love is light like a Thai meal, and every bit as
exotic
and healthy, beautiful and wholesome.
Your love is light like a jazz concert, so smooth and
ethereal it takes me to another land to another world. It
is wondrous to watch it unfurl.
Your love is light as the gentle caress which lets me
know
that you are the best.
Your love is light as the stroke of a hand always
spontaneous and never planned.
Your love is light like a short trip throughout a city and
the sites visited are so pretty, and to hear your
responses
that are so witty.
Your love is light like the wee hours of the morn, we
have
memories of last night and look forward for more.
Your love is light, pleasant, and free. Thank you for
sharing your love with me.

12-12-98

Who Are You?
(For Janet)

Who is this man in front of me? I am both fascinated
and cautious. I am attracted, yet I have set boundaries.
Who is this man and where is he from? What does he
believe and what are his words? What impact will he
make upon my life? Will it be as two souls uniting or
will it be like an automobile crash? What is his
purpose in my life and is it for good or for evil? He
seems honorable, but what is honor without honesty,
and how can I say he is honest if I do not know him?
His touch seems safe, but is his heart in the right
place? Are his motivations pure or am I the latest dish
on his menu? What say ye jury? Someone help me.
The man says he loved me, but how can I be sure? I
don't know what to do, so I ask, who are you?

12-12-98

My Sleeping Goddess
(For Janet)

She sits upon her couch in Mt. Olympus, her head
upon her hand on a warm night. Peaceful and serene is
her expression, her eyes are closed, and she has such a
beautiful smile upon her face. My black Mona Lisa
full of love and grace. How I long to press my lips
upon yours, but then the moment would be lost and the
peace disturbed. So I am satisfied just to observe.
What could you be dreaming about? An old lover
perhaps. A sunny day. A day at the beach, or watching
children at play. How I would love to step inside your
dreams to see; to hold you and love you, to run happy
and free. Though it is night your face beams radiant
with peace as you slumber upon your fine couch. Both
of us filled with fine wine and food of the Gods. My
stomach is filled with food, yet my heart is filled with
love for you. You have made a meal fit for a king and
I feel royal and pampered in your presence. How I
wish this night would not end and I could hold onto
you absorbing the warmth and beauty that are yours
alone. Sleep my dear goddess. Sleep, although we
have not touched, I have already loved you in my
dreams.

12-17-98

The Little Things
(For Karen)

It is the little things that draw me near. It is the little
things that make you dear. Things like hot tea and
honey so sweet. Things like a loving peck upon the
cheek. Things like the stroke of a thigh. Things like
the philosophical "why?" We sit upon your couch
discussing many things of this earth and beyond, of our
bodies and beyond. Yet in this cozy room and on your
comfortable couch, I feel the microcosm and the
macrocosm. The love in this room is as big as the love
in the universe and I feel my heart will explode not
from the big things; not from the powerful emotions,
but of the little things we share. A smile, a glance, a
touch, an embrace, the electricity and the chemistry of
you with me. So scientific, yet as simple as the joy
between a man and a woman. As I sit close to you
upon your couch in your studio, I feel the love not of
grandeur, pretentiousness and show; but of the quiet
simplicity of kindness, warmth and respect, the little
things that make up love.

12-17-98

Making A Memory
(For Jane E.)

Making a memory takes great care like taking a photograph. You want the right people, the right place, the right occasion. Making a memory can make us laugh or cry, desire life or die. Making a memory vivid is like giving it bright, powerful colors with heavy strokes. Making a memory last is like nurturing a growing plant, giving it love, tenderness, care, and remembering it, nurturing it. Making a loving memory is like an embrace and the warmth that is felt during that embrace and how you felt toward that person during the embrace. We can make all kinds of memories and in many different ways. I only hope the memories of you will always stay.

12-19-98

Following The Mothership
(For Oprah Winfrey)

I am following the mothership, wondering what the
plan will be. I am following the mothership trying to
chase destiny. I am following the mothership and
although the waves are high and I get tossed about, I
know she knows the path and will figure it all out. I am
following the mothership with the pain and strife. I
realize that this journey is what we call life; and
although the destiny is not clear, it is each day that
counts which make up the years. I am following the
mothership and all through the darkest nights we are
guided by the stars, their fixed presence gives stability
to our journey just as our father in the heavens gives
love and stability to our lives. Though the storms rage
and the wind blows, and all things seem for naught. It
is the mothership that has the master plan and helps us
through our doubt. Yes, I am following my mothership
as a duckling to her mother, my heart is filled with
hope, and my mind with endless wonder.

Kairos
(For Danae Alexander)

In time, in time all things happen in time; Kairos. I sit
and talk with you, wanting and desiring you to the
point of self-combustion—Kairos. I hold your hand
quietly and stroke it wanting to know every inch of it
like I want to know the rest of you—Kairos. I wait for
each word that comes out of your mouth, embracing it
and placing it in my memory, wanting even more for
my collection—Kairos. The desires come, but I must
push them away, the way the rocks withstand the sea—
yet even the rocks succumb to the passionate waves,
eventually—Kairos. Kairos is waiting for the right
time, the right place, the right person, and the right
reason. At this point in my life, you are what I need—
Kairos. As I kiss your cheek, yet desire more I wait,
not as a planner, not as a schemer, but as a lover and as
a dreamer. They say things come to those who wait,
well I wait, patiently—Kairos. Although this longing
for you will not go away, Kairos, Kairos, Kairos—they
will be fulfilled someday.

12-19-98

Inspiration
(For Jane E.)

Like a breath of fresh air you fill me. Like a campfire you give me warmth on the cold nights. Like a raging stream, you give excitement and refreshing coolness. Like a bright sunny day you show your brilliance. Like the ground I walk upon, you are firm, stable, and close to me. Like the four elements, you blend and make a complete person, a well balanced whole instead of fragmented pieces. I look up to you, although I am taller. I need your power, although I am stronger. I want your love because making love without love is empty love. I want just you, although I could have others. You are my inspiration, my breath of fresh air. You fill my lungs and give me peace. Your words of wisdom put me at ease. I am the poet, but you are my inspiration, you are the light in my darkness. You are the drink to quench my thirst. You are like food to my soul and what a splendid banquet you are. You are the consummate nurturer, for when I am near you, I hunger not. When I am with you, I thirst not. When I am with you, I have rest, I know peace, and last but not least, I am inspired.

12-14-98

Poems Of Light Written In Darkness
(For Marc R.)

In my most darkest hours come my most profound thoughts. Through the clouded vision and doubt, I find my way out; through words. In my most deepest and darkest despair, I found my ladder in my poems and with each poem I make my ascent from the darkness. Each poem is a rung which lifts me from the filth of negativity and hopelessness to the pure light of positive thinking and positive action. With my poems I am reaching out my arms to the father and begging him to lift me up. With my poems I am looking for my own personal North Star, the one that will take me to freedom; the poem of poems; the one that I write and will not have to write anymore. But alas that day has not come. The emotions that I cannot say, the words on the page convey. Those actions that I long to perform are in full motion in the form of a poem. With each word I am chipping at a chunk of marble, hoping to find myself underneath. The figure I create God only knows; but I pray he guides my hands with the words just right, to lead me out of the darkness and into the light.

12-24-98

My Gift Of Words
(For Cynthia)

My words are my gift to you on this eve of Christmas; and I fashion them the way the great elf fashions his toys for little girls and boys. My gifts are the feelings I have for you and the ease with which they spill upon the page. Like a Christmas piñata that has burst and spills sweet treats upon the ground, so my love for you pours out in the form of words, both spoken and written. Whether you are standing or sitting your appreciation enthralls me, fascinates me and goads me on to do more, to write even better than before; to speak with love as I never have before. Do you enjoy my gifts of words, I hope you do, because the inspiration is you. Your smile, your look, your thoughts, and your beauty which attracts and intrigues me. I want to be one with you and have our souls collide and exchange heartbeats, side by side. My words I give to you like packages of my heart, all for you. What a mixture you are. My sorceress. My goddess. The magic of love as well as the divinity of it spring forth from your very pores like an enchanting fragrance which beguiles and leads me on towards you, with my gift of words from the love of you.

12-24-98

Lay Your Head Upon Me
(For Cynthia)

Lay you head upon me, come take your rest. Come rest your weary heart with your head upon my chest. I know that you've been traveling with true love upon your mind, but the one that you deemed worthy is nowhere near or hard to find. Lay your head upon me and listen to the beating heart which belongs to you now and from the start. I say from the start for I was smitten when I first saw you. I say now for I feel the same crash inside my chest as my heart wants to leap out and fly to you. Lay your head upon my chest and slumber if you desire, and while you are in sweet slumber, I will tend the fire. The fire not of the hearth, but the fire of the heart; the fire of desire. Unlike the hearth flame which is only there for a moment in our lives, who's to say about the raging flame within my heart for you. It is as if it will always be, and lives eternal in me. Lay your head upon me and draw your strength as others have drawn their strength from you. Lay your head upon me and feast as others have feasted upon you. You have given so much, it is your turn to get. You have loved so hard, it is you who needs to be wet, to be nurtured, to be coddled and pampered. Lay your head upon me and take what you need, for you have already given enough to me.

12-24-98

You Feed Me
(For Cynthia)

The meals you prepare, so wholesome and good give
me strength and the energy to stand. A conversation
with you would stimulate any man. You feed me,
nourishing my mind and expanding it. Challenging it
for the finest of thoughts. You carefully select the
vegetables and meats for the optimum nutrition in the
same way you choose your words; so the ideas come to
fruition. The warmth and the taste of food stays with
me like a glowing furnace in my stomach, which
travels to my heart when I hear you speak. You feed
me, all of me, body and soul. From the exterior to the
inner most depths of my spirit, your nurturing ways
give rise to me and my anatomy. How fascinating you
are, and how unique, much like the numerous gourmet
dishes you prepared for me. What a delight to be in
your presence, as if you are an eight course meal in
front of me, a famished man, and I delight in eating
you whole. What a wondrous woman you are; light
and wholesome like your meals, yet with a touch of
spice which goes down very nice. What meal do you
prepare for me to see. It does not really matter,
whatever it is, you feed me.

12-24-98

Here In L.A.
(For Brianna, Brian, and Brandon)

Here I am in L.A., not much to do or to say. I arrived
on a plane yesterday. My nervousness abounds as I
drive through the outlying towns looking for a place
called Temecula, which is a heck of a way from
crowded L.A. Here I sit wondering what to do. So I
write, thinking of you. Will my kids love me or hate
me? Will they want to hug me or break me? Who's to
say? All I know is I'm here in L.A. I have many well
wishers back east, people who know me as a better
man than when I was a beast. Yes, I was a beast just a
few years ago when things did not work out, I had to
leave for Chicago. Although it is Christmas time in
Chicago with the bitter cold and snow, it is much
warmer there than in the L.A. that I now know. Even
though I am here for a few hours, I am wondering if
my visit will be sour. I can only give all that I have, if
that is not accepted, what else do I have. Although I
don't live for the approval of others, it would be nice if
we had unconditional love for each other. Here I am in
L.A. It is so sunny outside yet inside, I feel gray,
maybe it's my own smog that is getting in the way.

12-24-98

The Day Before Christmas
(For Jesus)

It is the day before Christmas and all through my mind
I am looking for a safe haven to find. A place to free
me from doubt, a place to feel okay, a place to tell me I
am accepted in all ways. It is the day before Christmas
and I want to shout. I want to release this bounding
love that wants a way out. To share with my brethren
not just the material things but hold onto the spiritual
ring which has no beginning or no visible end, it is the
joy of giving to stranger and friend. It is the day
before Christmas and my cup runneth over. I feel so
much love, I feel my body hover high above the earth,
feeling my true worth. I feel praise for my God and
oneness with the world; my love is expanding, like a
great flag unfurled, flying the banner of God's
unconditional love. On the day before his son's birth,
how God must have been filled with such joy and
mirth; Yet sadness and derision when you think of the
vision that in 33 years Jesus would shed tears and give
himself willingly on the cross to show the world that
his father is still the boss. What a Christmas gift for
me. Your death for my soul—thanks for setting us free.

12-24-98

On Holiday
(For Brianna, Brian and Brandon)

If there are any questions for me they have to wait. I
am on holiday. If there are any deeds that need to be
done, you must phone someone, but not me. I am free,
on holiday. If there are any worries or strife, stresses or
confusion, don't get the illusion I am there. I am on
holiday. If there are any emergencies, the world has
ended, or the apocalypse has come, that is all okay. I
am on holiday.

12-24-98

Give It Back
(For Janet)

Give me back my heart for you do not deserve it. You leave me deserted and empty wanting more and yet I have given all of me. Give me back my heart so that I may heal it. You have scarred and scratched it with your carelessness, and it is so valuable to me—the only one that I have, and I gave it freely to you. After so many years of protecting it, and nurturing it, and making it strong; I wanted you to have it. For your eyes only, for your touch only; and how did you respond, like a diffident, finicky cat. Some days enamored; some days aloof—yet I cared constantly with my love for you. It burned so bright like a fire in the night with a raging passion and a love for life. Yet words unspoken and distance have pushed us further from the important things. Things such as us and we, not I or me. When did we find out we were so far apart, apparently not until the breaking of this heart of mine, which I gave to you. Like a precious jewel in a silky sack, you don't deserve the gift, please give it back.

12-24-98

So I Pray
(For Dee)

I am not perfect Lord, so I pray. I miss the mark Lord, so I pray. I want to be near you Lord so I pray. I want clear thoughts Lord, so I pray. I am so lonely Lord, so I pray. Deliver me from my enemies Lord, so I pray. I need your warmth and love Lord, so I pray. I have trouble understanding Lord, so I pray. The world is so demanding Lord, so I pray. I need some understanding Lord, so I pray. I am hurting Lord, so I pray. I feel your omnipotent presence Lord, so I pray. I feel you in me Lord, so I pray. I want some wisdom Lord, so I pray. I need some guidance Lord, so I pray. I think I lost my way Lord, so I pray. I sinned today Lord, so I pray. I want to know you Lord, so I pray. I want to say "thank you Lord", so I pray. I want a better world Lord, so I pray. I want to be better Lord, so I pray. There are questions I must ask Lord, so I pray. You answered me Lord, so I pray. Amen.

12-24-98

This Is Your Day
(For Dee)

Oh my Lord, King of Kings this is the day to laugh and sing; giving praise to our wonderful Lord, the mighty savior from above. The one who came to break the chains and give our souls angel's wings. It is my God of whom I speak, three entities eternally. One of the father, one of the son, one of the spirit, 'till kingdom come. When mighty voice and trumpet blast the judgment call for men at last. To be before the mighty king to recount our lives, our works and deeds. To be concerned of what is in our hearts and minds and what we have wrought. Although by grace we come to thee, we need good works to make men free. What do we say to give you joy, what earthly actions do we employ to raise the mind and lift our souls, to restore our images to yours. Although we were made in your bright image, we have become so tarnished. We have strayed from your golden path; like errant sheep from their shepherdess. Help us Lord, draw us to you, let us remember today's meaning through and through.

12-26-98

Christmas Songs
(For Brianna, Brian and Brandon)

Angels' voices heard on high heralding that Christ is
nigh. What child is this that all love so in a little town
of Bethlehem. The silver bells ring so clear; do you
hear what I hear? For unto us a child is born, unto us a
son is given, let us remember this as we wish each
other a Merry Christmas. Noel, Noel, a sweet
Christmas song bringing joy to the world and asking
all to come who are faithful. As Jeanette Isabella
brings forth her torch, God rests ye merry gentlemen.
Good King Wenceslas, and the three kings of the
Orient are decking the halls and all notice the babe
away in the manger. Oh holy night, what a silent night
this will be, for there will be no white Christmas in
L.A. But it will be like a tender Tennessee Christmas.
It will be a blue Christmas without you, but I will try to
have a Feliz Navidad. Hallelujah and Amen.

12-26-98

Brianna

My first born. My only girl. How strong you are.
You are so expressive, so full of life. I am proud to be
your father. You have a rainbow in your smile and a
twinkle of the stars are in your eyes. Every day I am
around you, it is Christmas, because you are such a
precious gift. The music that you make brings a smile
to my face. I am so blessed to have you. You are my
little woman. Your walk is like a little princess. You
talk with such directness, as if you are throwing tiny
thunderbolts. You say what is on your mind and you
have plenty to say. You are so pleasant; you have a
way with words and putting them together like a string
of pearls, so beautiful and valuable. Like the sun on a
warm day, you share your warmth with the world and
the world loves you. Always be bright, think right, and
give your goodness to the world. You are a light on
this planet. Shine! Shine! Shine! You are Brianna,
my daughter. I love you.

12-26-98

Brian

My first son. So intelligent. You have a quiet strength
and a laser in your eyes. You give me joy with your
laughter and please me with your art. What kind of
future do you want? You may shape destiny if you
want. You may make history with your actions. Your
mind works overtime; thinking, dreaming, scheming.
You are so detailed, meticulous in your every action.
You strive for the best, to make perfection. You have
such drive and energy I am glad you are my son. The
Lord has blessed me so. You are able to make your
dreams appear out of thin air and put them down on
paper like a little magician. You are so tricky
sometimes. You choose your words carefully like a
soldier choosing his weapons; you want your words to
fit your thoughts. You are so caring about the world
and the environment. You love the earth and it loves
you back. Give to others and you will get back ten
times that amount. You are Brian, my first son. I love
you.

12-26-98

Brandon

My second son, but not second in my heart. You bring joy and laughter wherever you go. You have such a quick wit, yet you are a sensitive soul. You express your thoughts in a flash and you are not afraid to express your opinions. You are open and honest yet you do care about others and how they feel. You are so intense; so wise to be so young. Your brain is like a computer, forever reasoning, taking in data, analyzing it and striving for logical solutions. You also love to have fun. You ride the wind and are forever changing. One moment you are here, another moment you are there. You are constantly spreading your ideas, looking for a better way. You put things together, take them apart and put them together in your mind. Your brilliance is like flashes of lightning in the dark of night that brighten the sky. The world waits for your ideas. What will you think of next? You are Brandon, my second son. I love you.

12-26-98

The Bethel Prayer
(For Bethels Past, Present and Future)

May our love be unbroken the way our circle is unbroken. May your love for us be unbroken the way our love for you is unbroken. Let there be peace and love on this great sphere we call Earth. This is our prayer oh Lord.

Amen.

12-31-98

What Is The Color Of Justice?
(For World Peace)

How many people must die before we can see?
How much blood must be shed to see we all have red?
How much poverty must we see to know we all need
green?
How many times must we be burned to understand the
"white-hot" fire of prejudice?
How many times must we mourn to understand the
solemn color of black?
What is the color of justice—and if it exists will I ever
see
it, will I ever know it?
Why must others die due to the ignorance of others?
As I understand it, God made all men brothers.
When Jesus died was it only for the sins of the white?
When I pray will God hear me tonight?
Why should I worry of such "trivial" things?
I guess because prejudice and racism sting.
Why should I have to deal with this imperfect world?
What is the color of justice—
and if it exists, will I ever see it?
Will I ever know it?

The Birth Of A Goddess
(For Janet)

This is a special day for me, it is the birthday of my friend, my lover, my goddess, my queen. You are all of these things and much more to me. You fill me with adulation. You enhance my imagination, for I am constantly wondering what it would be like to be one with you. How smooth you are, how elegant, like the onyx stone or the black evening gown—you are class personified. You are the cog in my machine. You are the pattern in my quilt, and indeed you keep me quite warm. Warm not just in a physical sense, but the warmth from your emotions cannot be simplified or overlooked. You set my heart on fire and I am aflame for your love and I enjoy being consumed by you. I celebrate this day for it is a celebration of you, the total you, of that which is seen of those things done and those great things you have yet to do. With each year you only get finer, like wine, and I would be pleased to have a taste of thee. From the crown of your head to the tips of your toes, you are the woman for me. With a beautiful glance you extract the best from those around you, challenging them in your positive way. Defeat is not in your vocabulary, only patience and determination. Since you are a woman undeterred by circumstance and enhanced by adversity, I celebrate the start of your life and thank you for sharing some of it with me.

The Last Poem
(For Janet)

This is the last poem you will see. This is the poem that sets me free. Without anger or malice, this poem is the golden chalice, the one I want you to cherish, the one that is unblemished. All poems tie into this one; of all the pain, and all the fun. The bittersweet taste of a relationship—the ups and downs, the highs and lows, the summer's suns and the winter's snows. What a season we have had in each other's life, and I will treasure it always as an old photograph in a tattered album. The memory of you will be permanently etched upon my brain like profound words etched in marble, and the profound words would be "I love you." How can I end something which never began? You see the illusion was all in my mind and what a grand illusion it was—for awhile. But alas, with all illusions, the truth will find its way through it and as a fire rages through delicate paper, the truth has blazed into my mind. What ecstasy I knew in your arms. Although it was short lived, your memory will haunt me to my grave, but what a beautiful spirit you are.

12/2002

My Sugar
(For Lady A)

Though small in size your heart is so big and grand. Your femininity makes me twice the man. Dark and sweet like chocolate. A radiant smile like a beacon guiding the ships to shore you guide me to a better place, a safe haven. How my ship longs to rest in your harbor. I enjoy resting in your arms feeling the warmth of you and enjoying the sweet smell of you. You are my sugar. So sweet, addictive and enticing you add life to the senses-like sugar.

7/10/03

Searching For Uranium
(Or 16 words)

I asked my leader "Where do I find Uranium?"
He said "ask the British"-who said "Look in Africa."
I asked my leader "Where do I find Weapons Of Mass Destruction?"
He said "Look in Iraq."
I asked my leader "Where do I find Saddam?"
He said "Look in Iraq, maybe Syria."
I asked my leader "Where do I find Osama?"
He said "Look in Afghanistan, maybe Pakistan."
I asked my leader "Where do I find the TRUTH?"
He said "I cannot help you with that one."
     "You have to find that out for yourself!"

12/2002

My Chocolate Qüeen
(For Lady A)

Sweet tender kisses in the night. Your toothy smile
illuminates the darkness. Your Ebony skin reminds me
of one soft and tasty chocolate bar. I enjoy stroking
your long silky hair as I enjoy stroking your short curly
hair. I enjoy the ambrosia of your mouth as if I were
being refreshed at an oasis. I enjoy kissing the sweet
dew of love from your enlarged rose petals. How you
make me long for your sweet embrace. How I long to
give you the big O and how you tease me from giving
it to you. You are my Major Sugar! And I stand at
attention waiting for your next command. You are my
Queen Bee and how I love being one of your royal
subjects.

All hail to the Queen who gives us sustenance.

12/02

Cupid

There you go shooting me in the butt again. Damn
you, you little bastard flying around with your bow and
arrow wreaking havoc in peoples lives and disturbing
their mundane existence.
Damn you for making me feel again when I was
resigned to a life of loneliness.
Damn you for making me want to go out when I was
content to be home—by myself.
Damn you for depleting my funds by buying expensive
gifts and fancy dinners.
Damn you for making me intoxicated over this new
woman when I haven't gotten over the other woman
yet.
Yes, Cupid you are a bastard. But without you, life
would not be as exciting and love would be just
another crude four-lettered word.

12/24/02

If Jesus Were Black
(For Trent Lott & Strom Thurmond)

If Jesus were black would you still pray or be an
atheist forever and a day. What about "hair of wool"
or "feet of bronze," the Bible writers could not be
wrong. What should I care, if God is love, and God is
everywhere. I care! I care! Yes I do when pictures
are painted depicting Christ as a Caucasian. People
say don't be a racist and then I say who has seen Christ
or the disciples faces. If people have not seen then
how can they draw – the most important figure since
Jehovah. When Mary and Joseph ran to hide why
didn't they go north if Christ were white. Could you
hide a white man in the blackness of Harlem? I guess
you would have to ask Bill Clinton that. Oh yeah, one
last thing before I go. Look at a map or look at a
globe. Find Israel, which is closer, Northern Europe or
Africa – I rest my case.

1/03

The Bed
(For Lady A)

I did not know the bed could be used as a musical
instrument until you taught me.
I did not know you could make it hum.
I did not know you could make it whine.
I did not know you could make it cry, like the sizzling
strings on a guitar or have the refinement and class of
the violin or the brash roughness of a harmonica or the
tenderness of a harp.
You are teaching me this new instrument, and I love
you for it. Like a conductor you know the right
movement to get the right sound and I follow through
with my instrument to play that note just right so you
can get that high note that we've been searching for.

2/03

Like a Baby
(For Lady A)

You are so tender – like a baby.
You are so soft – like a baby.
You are so smooth – like a baby.
I love the way you coo when I make love to you
    like a baby.
I love the way you giggle when I make you wiggle
    like a baby.
I love the way you squeal when I give that special feel
    like a baby.
I love the way you twist and turn crawl & squirm
    like a baby.
I love the way you reach out with love to embrace me,
all trusting, all loving – like a baby.
I love when you flash that satisfied all knowing smile
that shows total contentment – like a baby.

2-11-03

Riding the Crest
of the Wave
(For Alan)

Have you ever wondered about those people who
never seem to have a worry or never seem to have a
care? Always up to the challenge, always taking the
dare. High above the crowd they travel with a smile
upon their face, riding the crest of the wave with grace
and confidence from place to place. Did you ever
worry about "what would happen if…" or totally
hesitate and want to quit. Then you turn around with
an awestruck gaze to one of your companions riding
the crest of the wave. He does not even care and could
not give a damn, yet he rides the wave, solves the
problem and lands flawless on the sand.

Tony Bethel

2-14-03

Lady A

To the little lady with the impish grin, thanks for letting me come in. Into your mind, into your heart, you have given my spirit a brand new start. The power in your thighs does not even compare to the power of your mind or the depth of love in your heart. You are unique. From the time of our first meeting you opened yourself to me and welcomed me in and what a hostess you have been. You have fed me physically, intellectually, emotionally and spiritually. What is left? You make me regret seeing the sun. For our nights of endless passion makes me want to stop the world and prolong the love, reverse the earth's rotation and start the day again and again.

The 168th Hour
(For Massage Therapists)

24 hours a day 7 days a week the 168th hour approaches. Each week they look forward to the touch that will heal their ills. Each week they look forward to telling me of triumphs and sorrows, of physical joy and physical pain. I twist, shape and knead their bodies and they wait patiently for that 168th hour. This is the moment that they may get away from their worries, from their spouses, from their children, from the world. This time is as precious as it is holy. They lie upon the altar and I rebuild their temples physically, intellectually, emotionally and spiritually. Everyone is different and each has a different complaint. As a priest in a confessional I listen carefully, quietly; not judging but loving unconditionally as I am loved unconditionally. The 168th hour approaches the end – leaving rest, relief, refreshment and anticipation for the next 168th hour.

Anatomy of Racism

I saw two children playing happily on the beach, one
white, one black, one male, one female and I wondered
at what point will they learn to hate each other?
Will it be their parents that mention the "evils" of the
other?
Will it be the influences of their sisters or brothers?
Will it be their "friends" who intend to deceive?
Will it be their churches that say it is "God's will" and
destiny?
Will it be the unfeeling pressure of society intertwined
with its
hypocrisy?
At what point do we feel that one must dominate the
other to win?
If two children so beautiful as these should grow up in
such
a racist society, would it not be better for them to swim
out of reach, and their dead bodies be washed upon the
beach,
one black, one white, in each other's arms, both dead
to this world—yet free in the next.
As Christ died to save our souls
Must children die to save humanity?

Tony Bethel

12/00

No Excuses

I am black. No excuses.
I am white. No excuses.
I am a woman. No excuses. I am a man. No excuses.
I am poor. No excuses. I have my own troubles. No
excuses.

No excuse for hatred of those we have never met.
No excuse to rob when we may ask for what we need.
No excuse for violence when we have the power to
discuss our troubles.
No excuse to humiliate others if we are all God's
children.
No excuse not to help others if we have enough for
ourselves.

We must share this planet – no excuse for trashing it.
We do not live here alone – no excuse for being rude.
We all have dreams and desires – no excuse for
discouraging others for their aspirations.
We all need to live – no excuse for not providing food,
water, shelter, clothes and jobs – if you have the means
to do so.

It is not welfare, it is humanity.
I am too smart to be racist. I am too busy to hate.
I have no time for fools.
No excuses!

Tony Bethel

12/00

Gold, Silver And Green

I did not ask to be black – but here I am.
You did not ask to be white – but there you are.
Me hating you, you hating me. Why?
History perhaps?
I say no, it is about color; not black nor white
but of my favorite three: Gold, Silver and Green.
It is so funny how similar in spelling the words green
and greed.
It is greed that brought my people here from Africa.
It is greed that caused genocide against the Native
Americans as well as Jews and Arabs.
It is greed that brought the people of Asia, Mexico
and Europe as cheap laborers.
It is greed that caused the Civil War,
Do you hate me because of my color, or the fact
that I am free and you cannot make money
off of me; or that I compete with you in
all areas of life as well as making a living.
It is funny how money makes the most serious
racist a hypocrite. Yes, it is about color
Gold, Silver and Green.

Tony Bethel

Day by Day
(for Lady A)

Deep, rich, smooth and sweet, like the most expensive chocolates you are a delight to me. How I enjoy holding you and kissing you. I do not want to let go but be inside you forever. How could two bodies move so effortlessly, as if they were one. Your love is so magical and mysterious you give real meaning to life. Beyond the materialism, beyond the hypocrisy I wish to love you endlessly. The softness of your skin is so addictive to my touch. Your perfume intoxicates me with passion and endless desire for you. I want you for all time and I am so glad that you are mine. At any point you could be free, yet you stay, showing your undying loyalty. I owe you so much and how I enjoy paying you back—day by day.

One Man In A Million
(For the Million Man March)

Don't judge me by the color you see,
because you are looking at a human being.
Don't judge me by the features of my face,
because I am a member of the human race.
There is just *one race*, The human race.

Don't ask me if I'm black or white,
I might be either one tonight.
Don't lay any "guilt trips" on me.
I am not responsible for history.
I am a human being, I have a right to be free.

Don't try to erase who I am because I do not
fit into your plans.
I have a right to be here too, just as much, maybe
more than you.

Don't try to take my life – get one of your own.
Don't rob me of my land and then call it home.
Don't criticize the way I pray – God understands
what I say.
Don't put me down for who I am.
I am a human.
I am a man.

1/1/00

Millennium at Two
(For The Future)

Millennium at two, my have you grown.
So much different than one.
From the Middle Age to New Age.
From the printing press to the computer.
You have gotten quite smart over the years
and yet still stubborn with our wars,
and discord and genocide, I guess old habits are tough
to break.
From the crusades to communism. From reformation
to evangelism.
From isolation to globalization.
From world exploration to space exploration.
From sparseness to overpopulation.
From horsepower to nuclear power.
From the microcosm to the macrocosm.
Since your first birthday you have seen one thousand
years,
one thousand tears, one thousand hopes and one
thousand fears.
Where do we go from here? The future is anyone's
guess,
with world domination a constant quest.
Capitalism is running strong and hard as the bull
tramples over the lower classes.
Should we look for a brave new world or for big
brother?

Tony Bethel

1/17/00

One Bullet, One Life

How could something so small and meaningless
destroy such potential.
Life is so precious, so beautiful, so valuable, yet the
crack of a weapon
can send a bullet to end that life. All the hopes, all the
dreams, all the
could be into never will. The cold emotionless blue
metal of the bullet
ironically matches the cold lifeless bluish tint of the
dead body. Although
it takes a weapon to give a bullet life, it's life is short
lived as it
pierces through the heart of an unsuspecting victim. It
is as if the bullet
envies the life of the person and once the victim falls
dead, the bullet
may also rest. How can something worth just a few
cents deplete something
as valuable as a human life. They say life goes on, and
indeed it does for
the victims families, like the hollowness and emptiness
of the hollow point
bullet.

Tony Bethel

5/07/00

My River
(For Joann)

Oh what a beautiful river I have. The water tastes so
sweet, so clean. How I love to be in you and how
refreshed my body feels when I am in you. I feel
purified. I feel blessed. I love the depths of you and
the way you wind and turn and twist. I love to feel the
softness of the river banks between my fingers. The
fish love to race deep inside of you, they sense your
nurturing and your love. I love it when your waters rise
and flow and flow and flow. I love your wetness. I
love putting my face upon you and to swim in your
depths. So deep, so mysterious, to be inside of you is
an adventure and a mystery. I love it when my boat is
upon thee. How you rock and sway. The ride is so
beautiful – I wish it would never end. If I could just
stay upon you forever. I love the way your waters
caress my boat as I sail upon you, sometimes tightly,
sometimes loosely, but at all times with love. As the
sun goes down upon you the moon rises and I too rise
in my boat upon thee. Sailing deep within thee you
feel endless. You are like the Nile my African queen.
How warm you are, you give life to all that you touch.
I enjoy the night being upon you, the perfect end to a
perfect day. I love the way you open up to me as I
come into you from the sea.

5/27/00

Jeanette

Such a delicate name for such a strong person. How
mysteriously open you are. A contrast between light
and darkness, between innocence and seduction. I am
magnetized by you and yet I feel your boundaries.
You are so enticing and yet you are unto yourself. I
enjoy the softness of you, your tenderness. Your sweet
perfume draws me to you like a butterfly and how I
love to be inside your beautiful flower. How sweet
your taste and your wetness refreshes me like the
morning dew – must I leave inside of you. Your hair is
so dark and thick and strong, yet your skin is so soft,
supple and sensuous. I am addicted to touching you.
How I love to glide my hands upon thy thighs, your
lightness makes me high like the air sign that you are –
Gemini.
You are like two people: one, secretive and
mesmerizing, filling me with intense desire. The other,
open, honest, intelligent, funny and friendly to the
world. Two women in one body – could a man ask for
more? Your eyes remind me of the brightness of the
sun, which is matched by the warmth of your heart.
Feliz Cumpleaños, mi amor.

2-14-03

My Special Valentines
(To the Residents of Misericordia)

My special valentines: from your wild laughter to your
crooked smiles your unconditional love drives me
wild. You ask for nothing but give the world. I can
feel your warmth unfurl as a flag waving in the breeze.
I feel your warmth like the sun beaming down on me.
Though some bodies are twisted they move with the
joy of life. Though some are confused it does not stop
the moments of wit and unique wisdom. Though some
have medical problems it does not stop the human
spirit – which is limitless. You are all special in your
own way.

I wish you all love this Valentine's Day!

12/02

Infidelity

One woman two men, two women one man it's all
equal, its all sin. Three into two will never do. So
many people yet one person always comes up short.
Either in their heart or in the mind, love can be so
unkind. She puts people in your life at different times
but sometimes the sequence is out of line. Sometimes
we care when we should let go. Sometimes we do
things we know are no-nos. Why can't these things be
pre-arranged. We could save so many broken hearts
before Valentine's Day. Why can't we say what needs
to be said *before* we end up in another lover's bed.
Why is it so difficult to let go. Why can't we tell old
lovers what they need to know? Instead we both tell
each other lies until it stinks and draws those ugly flies.
The flies of Deception, Envy, Jealousy and
Possessiveness. The flies of Aggression, Neglect,
Abuse *and* Infidelity.
When a relationship fails its like a pile of excrement
that must be picked up, but no one wants to do it. No
one wants to take the responsibility but then things
fester and stink to the high heavens. We then look with
our eyes and see the aforementioned flies, gleefully
picking at the fetid mess, until even the hope of a
decent friendship is devoured. I forgive you and ask
the same of me of that fly called infidelity.

11/01/01

Sailing Through Souls
(for All Souls' Day)

As I walk down the crowded corridor I find myself
sailing through a sea of souls. I feel the personalities
crash around me like the waves upon the ocean. I can
feel the cold stares as the cold wind in the North
Atlantic. I see some friendly smiles and they are
calming like the gentle breezes of the Caribbean; and
then I see blank expressions with the vastness of the
Pacific. Each soul I encounter is like a body of water
and I feel myself sailing, at times even fighting the
current of their resistance. Some people yielding, while
others stand with stiff defiance like the Rock of
Gibralter sitting at the entrance of the Mediterranean.
As I wander, I wonder about these bodies I am passing
through and if I will see them again; and if I see them
will I remember them or they me. Water is so versatile.
It may be hard as steel in the form of ice or it may be
as light and nebulous as the clouds or as flowing and
lyrical as the ocean. So versatile, yet it is still water.
We too share such diversity. So different, yet so
human. So constant, regardless of the variable sea of
bodies and emotions each one has a soul.

5/02/03

Paint Me The Color Of Peace
(For the World)

Paint me the color of peace and maybe there will not
be such hatred. Paint me the color of peace and maybe
there will not be such fear. Paint me the color of peace
and there will be no tears. Paint me the color of peace
and there will be such happiness. But there is no color
of peace, just the color I was born with, and why
should *that* be an issue? Who in their mother's womb
chose to be the color that they are? Color is a given
like our body type or genes. Yet it is color which
elicits one of the most violent of responses. It is ironic
that the darkness of human behavior has no correlation
with color – there is evil and good in all groups. I
pondered the differences in color and I believe it is a
personal test, as is all of life. For those of you who
have not seen God—how can you hate your brother or
sister who you now see. What is the color of God? I
say the color of peace.

9/1999

Three Boys Wrapped In Orange
(For Northern Ireland)

The color of fire is yellow. The color of blood is red.
Yellow and red is orange. How ironic, orange is such
a pretty color, the color of the sunset on a beautiful
day. Yet the color of orange has become tainted.
Three babes will not see the bright orange sun again or
feel its warmth.
How ironic, such a positive color could lead to such
pain.
Must we go through this senseless violence again and
again.
One man Protestant, one woman Catholic, who did
they hurt.
What was their sin to lose three boys who will not
become men?
Tell me something, is the Christ of the Protestant the
same as the
Christ of the Catholic? Is the Christ that died for Peter
the same as the Christ of Luther?
Please tell me what did I miss, or am I asleep as the
apostles
were in Gethsemane? Since when did religion
supercede compassion?
Since when did hatred supercede love? Since when
did traditions
of men supercede the words of Christ?
Since when was orange the color of pain instead of
happiness?

Tony Bethel

Three boys wrapped in orange – lost, but not forgotten.
Just as the orange sun sinks into the sea giving way to
the
darkness of night; it rises again with the hope of a new
day.
Let us keep the hope to outshine the darkness.

2/03

Bright Star
(For Michael P. Anderson)
(and the other Columbia astronauts)

You are our bright star shining so brightly in the heavens.
Your accomplishments are as stellar as your beaming smile.
So many placed their hopes in you and you did not fail them.
Although you are first and foremost an astronaut; you are one of us, and how proud we are of you. How unfortunate your untimely death would come during Black History month. Yet, the time of your death will be firmly chronicled and preserved for future generations as our "bright star" during the month of February. During this month you are the embodiment of what both Malcolm and Martin were talking about. You definitely had your passport to the future with your educational accomplishments and your content of character is above question. You truly personify those statements. You are a true American with your teamwork and leadership. You are the perfect example of what Black people in this country may accomplish if given the opportunity. How proud I am of you. You are the ultimate Black male. May your constellation shine brightly as the North Star, leading your people with science and technology.

2/03

There Are No Niggers Here.
(For Black History Month)

From Algeria to Madagascar there are no niggers here.
From Zaire to Kenya there are no niggers here. From
Egypt to South Africa there are no niggers here. Land
of the Pharaohs, land of higher math, land of ancient
mysteries, land of Hannibal, birthplace of scholars and
kings, there are no niggers here. Adored by ancient
philosophers, desired for her beauty, mother Africa
you are both wise and beautiful beyond compare. The
birthplace of the human race and the nurturer of man,
mother Africa I sing of your greatness again and again.
I am proud to be a son of thee. No niggers as far as the
eye can see. To the heights of Kilamanjaro to the
lowest valley all that I see are beautiful people that
look like me. Some darker, some lighter, descendants
of warriors, of fighters, people refusing to be
dominated, people of promise, people of elation. How
colorful we are in full African garb. How expressive
are our eyes when we tell a story or give an
explanation. How sensual we are when we perform our
dances. How persistent we are when we notice
injustice. How driven we are when we have a
worthwhile goal. How loving we are when we are with
our families. A culture so rich, a culture so free, I am
so proud to be a descendant of thee. No niggers there,
no niggers in me.

2/03

More Than Black
(For Black History Month)

I refuse to be a one dimensional stereotype picture on a page, I am more than that, more than Black.
Since when was a human being supposed to be limited by their own color as to what to say, think, eat and drink. I don't buy that, I can't accept that, I am more than that – more than Black.
I refuse to let others tell me who I can see or who my friends are to be. I cannot accept that destiny because I am light years beyond that, not looking back, much more than that – more than Black.
I abhor others telling me what I should wear or how to speak, when ignorance is what they reek –- that foul, stinking, stench of racism, that's not for me. Not in this life or in the next, because I am more than that, yet I am all of that, Phat and more. I am past the door, past the gate, destiny awaits and I refuse to be late, because I am better than that – I am more than Black.
I cannot sit and wait for a label of this or a label of that, because I can only be defined by me, which in turn is myself – is that confusing, it is meant to be because you see I am more than that – more than Black. Beyond the bell curve, beyond the statistics, beyond the teeny tiny minds that try to limit me – I will be free, and all of that, because I am more, so much more than Black.

11/2/98

The Breast
(To All Women)

Its roundress and softness amazes me, a feat in
engineering by the great designer in the sky. So supple
and pliable, how I love to touch it, caress it and stroke
it. I love to rub the nipples between my finger tips and
see them swell. God is such a genius. Two mounds
like twin hills on a fertile plain. I love to put my mouth
upon them, how I envy children. I feel so secure when
my mouth is upon them. I feel I am experiencing a
nutritious treat, so warm, so sweet, I laugh at the way
the nipple pops in and out of my mouth. I feel so safe
here. I could lay my head here for hours and just listen
to your heart beat. It feels so natural here, as though I
belong, and although they come in all sizes, shapes and
colors it is yours I enjoy. Although they do not
determine the woman, the heart underneath them
definitely determines the woman. In many cases the
size on top does not determine the size of the heart
below. There is such a spiritual quality to them, almost
sacred, since children are nourished there. Women are
not only the bearers of life they are also the sustainers
of life and how I enjoy the sustenance. As I lay my
head upon your bosom and feel the warmth of it and
hear the heartbeat below like a sensual metronome
keeping the rhythm of life, I feel at peace with myself,
with you, with the world.

10/13/02

Friday the 13th
(For The Superstitious)

You come along every few months and sneak up on us
with your bad luck and bad timing. You make us
careful and fearful wondering what will happen within
those 24 hrs. You make us wonder is it you or is it us.
You are often a scapegoat for our mistakes, be they
intentional or unintentional. Bad luck for some, good
luck for others. Friday the 13th, what does it really
mean? Is it just another day of cobwebs, spiders and
black cats; or is it an opportunity to overcome our
fears, prejudices and ignorance. Friday the 13th you
come ever so often to remind us as humans of our
frailty, of our dark side, of our belief in the
supernatural; and that of the other world, the other side
– the untried. You remind us of the unknown and
unsaid, the occult and the mystery. Friday the 13th is
it truth or fallacy, fact or fiction. Some will say yes
others no. Who really knows because with good comes
bad and vice versa. Is it the things we've actually
experienced or what we have rehearsed. What is really
true, goblins, gnomes, fairies or what about real life
which is even more scary. Friday the 13th, it comes
every few months and catches us sleeping, then makes
us alert to each incident that happens on that day and
we are left with the possibility of what if, and from
what if to why and it all comes down to what do you
believe. Is it bad luck or bad decisions? Is it a black cat
across your path or a black cloud in your life. Is it you

or somebody else. In reality, it comes back to me and responsibility for what I say and do. Friday the 13th yes, but the ultimate choice is mine.

12/12/02

The Black White man
(For Mr. Thomas)

Who am I and why all this confusion; I hate to live in
such an illusion – looking in the mirror seeing black
but inside feeling white. Why do I hate myself so.
Was it something they taught me or was it something I
taught myself. When does ambition become selling
out. When does cultural diversification become
abnegation. When does integration become being like
them rather than being yourself with them. What about
cultural identification, something that is splitting this
nation. What is the big deal if something is black or
white as long as it is a good idea. Right? Wrong.
Racism lives and is very strong. It twists the most
innocent of motives and puts us all down. How can a
few people be used to blame a whole race. History can
be written with numerous faces and the one holding the
gun is the one with the pen. History is written by the
victors – not ordinary men. Maybe that is where the
confusion lies, when you begin to believe the lies you
are told in school and falsely conclude, your race is
doomed. Again I say who writes history is not the
ordinary man. It is the slave owner not the slave. It is
the ship that is tossed by the waves to-and-fro, and
only the waves know where the ship will go.
Sometimes I feel much like that ship set on my course
but tossed around by unseen forces. My identity I am
trying to find – just a Black White man marching in
time.

The Myth

Tell me the myth of the Black man, the one where he is
on dope because he can't cope because he lost hope.
Tell me the myth of the Black man, the one where he's
got to steal so he can have a meal so he's got to cut a
deal.
Tell me the myth of the Black man, the one where he's
so lazy because he's too stupid or crazy or he's drunk,
dope addict or his brain is hazy.
Tell me the myth of the Black man, the one where he's
such a big stud but as a father he is a dud and he drags
his woman through the mud.
Tell me the myth of the Black man, the one where he is
always poor going from door to door. Always wanting
more or trying to chase a "whore" or lying intoxicated
on the floor.
Tell me the myth of the Black man the one where he
goes to his honey and is begging for some money
because he can't manage his own and is always asking
for a loan.
Tell me the myth of the Black man, the one where he is
always blaming the white man for his woes, and that
all white people are his foes and how he would like to
break the white man's nose.
Tell me myths all day long some weak, some strong,
obscuring the truth, confusing the youth. Until they
grow up and tell their children and then the cycle is
complete the carousel goes around and around never
stopping – like a hellish nightmare, yet lived by us.

Tony Bethel

Tell me the myth of the Black man because I need a good laugh today and then maybe through the laughter you will see the tears and understand all of your unfounded fears; which led to the tyranny that imprisons you as well as me. Understand the myth is just a lie you tell and when you realize that perhaps you may break its spell.

5/13/99

For Bonnie D.

My hands caress the soft round contours of your body.
The hills, the valleys, the plain. How natural you are.
I feel the warmth externally and internally. Your light
shines through your body like a prism and illuminates
me. Your sweetness is like the sweet rich taste of
honey and oh so natural. How fortunate I am to have
my hands upon you and How fortunate I am to be in
this profession, where my touch energizes and I in turn
am energized by you.

Thank you

Tony

MY WAR

DIARY

"…the lies get deeper,
yet I am my brothers keeper"
—Tony Bethel

3/17/03

48 Hours

48 Hours the clock is ticking
48 Hours the world is aching.
48 Hours time to grieve.
48 Hours my heart is on my sleeve.
48 Hours tears are flowing like a river.
48 Hours the day of reckoning is drawing nearer.
48 Hours you should have disarmed by now.
48 Hours Innocents blood will flow.
48 Hours what cowards you are.
48 Hours civilians will suffer most by far.
48 Hours, 2 days, 2 countries, 2 men, 2 ideologies
Too blind to see.
War will not benefit anyone
least of all *our* country.

3-18-03

For God and Country
In memory of Capt. Ryan A. Beaupre and
other soldiers of Operation Iraqi Freedom

For God and country they come and join.
For God and country the fire is in their loins.
For God and country we must set them free.
For God and country and democracy.
For God and country we endure the desert heat.
For God and country our forces are in the hot seat.
For God and country we are willing to die,
as our loved ones can only standby and cry.
For God and country we will defeat our foes.
For God and country my heart the Lord knows.
For God and country we try to make a better life.
For God and country, for our husband or wife
For God and country we will stand firm and tall.
For God and country we will answer the call.
For God and country we do these things in hopes that
one day, throughout the world, freedom will ring.

Lt. Tony Bethel, USNR
Operation Desert Storm

3-19-03

Eight O'clock

Eight o'clock the time has come.
Eight o'clock my body's numb.
Eight o'clock what shall we do.
Eight o'clock Iraq we shall renew.
Eight o'clock some bombs have already fallen.
Eight o'clock America's reputation has fallen.
Eight o'clock their troops surrender to us.
Eight o'clock their people cheer us.
Eight o'clock at the border of Kuwait.
Eight o'clock we are opening the gate.
Eight o'clock we are coming in.
Eight o'clock we are going to win.
Eight o'clock we warned you before.
Eight o'clock we are now at your door.
Eight o'clock no more words to say.
Eight o'clock now our weapons converse today.
Eight o'clock victory will be ours.
Eight o'clock it is now our hour.

3-20-03

A Shower of Bombs

When I think of a shower I think of cleansing.
When I think of a shower I think refreshing.
When I think of a shower I think peaceful.
When I think of a shower I think restful.
A shower has come to Iraq.
A forced shower.
A shower that is given to a stubborn, willful, dirty child.
A forced but necessary shower.
I see a shower of bombs coming from the sky.
I see American justice raining from on high.
I see a shower of tears from Iraqi eyes.
I know in my heart that some innocent will die.
Will this American shower cleanse Iraq of its dirty leadership?
Will the Iraqi people be refreshed after this American shower?
Will the American shower bring peace to a troubled people?
Will the Iraqi people finally have rest?
Only time will tell.

3-21-03

An Infection of "Peace"

Securing areas in the south moving to the north.
City-by-city an infection has come forth.
Small American flags are symptoms of the disease.
Many Iraqi soldiers have given up with ease.
Does an easy war make it right?
Is it due to fear they avoid the fight?
A few casualties today, Americans and British
were slain.
The captain that died just lived a few miles away.
People there seem happy to see, the slow liberation of
their country.
More of our troops add to the infection.
while more of their troops increase defection.
We are moving in like a quick cancer and the regime
of Saddam Hussein will have to answer.
Two other marines were also killed today.
A price to pay for America's way.
So young, so brave – will America forget the sacrifices
they gave? I won't!
Will America forget the lives they have saved?
I won't!
Will this American infection of "democracy" take out
the evils of tyranny?
Who is next in the "axis of evil"?
Is it Iran or North Korea?
An infection of "peace" awaits.

3/22/03

From the Heart

Cities are falling like dominoes.
We are steadily defeating our foes.
Fires are sprouting all over the place.
I see the look of determination in these young faces.
We now have casualties:
of ourselves, our allies and the enemy.
Casualties on the land and in the air.
What is happening just doesn't seem fair.
With futures bright and hearts aglow these young
heroes come to fight our foes.
Despite the political intricacies,
they make it simple – "people got to be free".
What happens now is anyone's guess, as pride fills our
loved ones chest.
But sadly enough reality shows and slowly, so slowly
our
casualties grow. Whether you are for or against
this war of ours, know this – our troops fight from
the heart.

3/23/03

In Shock and Awe

More resistance is met today.
An easy enemy goes away.
What we see now is a stiffening will, but we continue
to push up that hill.
Though casualties increase – some self-inflicted.
The ire of the world is now affected.
People rise up from around the world to demonstrate
against this controversial war.
Captives have been taken today. POW's that we
must save. Men & women of valiant strength.
Let us pray that the Lord gives the will to endure this.
Things that seem easy just aren't so.
An ally at the northern border tries to overflow.
Rumors about Saddam fly as fires burn into the
desert sky.
A war thought easy may have to be rethought.
Easy answers for difficult questions are sought.
Regardless of the political intrigue,
our men and women strive to make the world free.

3/24/03

Things Are Different!

Things are not as we thought they would be, more
resistance as we fight the Iraqis. Pockets of resistance
pop up like brush fires. To get this over with and go
home is our desire. So many things to coordinate.
From helping those in Basra to fighting those in
Nasiriyah. And lets not forget Umm Qasr and the
Fedayeen, the fighting now has turned mean. So many
faceless heroes fighting to defeat our foes. Back home
we are divided.
Yet those on the front lines know why they are
fighting. Things aren't as they were before, this time it
seems more like a war. There are things we didn't
have before like POWs and a traitor soldier.
How did things come to this, yet, we stay the course to
finish the mission.
As we drag through another day it appears things are
different, the war has changed.

3/25/03

Sandstorms

Sand, sand everywhere, beneath their feet and in the
air. Blown around it looks unreal, they really don't
know what to feel. The distances they cannot judge.
They are bogged down like in thick mud. The storms
remind me of both the confusion and illusion; of what
we thought and of what we know; of what is dead and
what we are trying to grow. We want to plant the seeds
of freedom but what a tough row to hoe. I see the sand
storms and the surreal glow of the sun. I think of Van
gogh's "Starry Night" and the parallels that run.
We are there for a purpose though the world is
confused. Let us hope our troops are not being used.

3/26/03

Sitting On The Sidelines
(Truly March Madness)

Almost 500 Iraqi soldiers died today. What a great
battle – I should be happy. But they have some of our
troops and this war is not over – I now feel crappy.
We sit on the sidelines like at a game. Yet though we
see the faces we don't know the names. So many of
our young ones are there. They cherish their country
showing no fear. The fighting continues hour upon
hour. Yet when I get tired of watching I can get up and
take a shower. Yet the war continues while I am in the
warmth of my home. I wish the man upstairs I could
phone.

   I would say "Lord please end this and bring our
troops home."

3/27/03

At A Standstill

Rapid progress that was made
now seems to slowly fade. Nasiriyah and Basra
won't give in,
but soon we will have more men. POW's are
still being held, while back at home
powerful emotions are being felt. Why are we here
some say.
Yet others say we must pave the way.
America, we are at a standstill. Yet we still
climb this daunting hill. Obstacles in our path
we surmount them with a grim laugh. Yet
resistance slowly comes, making the joints
and mind numb.
I still don't know how to feel.
I guess my heart still stands still.

3-28-03

America Right Or Wrong?

Attacking us like army ants they hit and run
and block our path.
I hear rumors of Iran and Syria joining the fray.
Come one, come all and join the party.
Will this be just us and Iraq or will we have the
whole Arab world on our back.
Who can we *not* trust today.
It seems our allies sometimes get in the way.
Do we have to adjust our strategy?
Are we fighting in accordance with reality?
And still our POWs are being kept.
I turned my head and Jesus wept.
Now the U.N. wants to have a say.
They were no where in sight when we went
our way. There is so much going on but we must
remain strong.
America right or wrong you are my country
through and through.
There is just one thing I ask. Treat these
troops as heroes when they get back.

3/29/03

We Pause

It is time to pause to think about our cause.
Have the Iraqis broken any laws?
They are fighting a force greater than their own.
The tactics they are using makes me want to groan.

It is time to pause to think about our cause.
Have we broken any laws?
To liberate those who need to be free, yet no one called
on me. But it *is* up to us, it *is* our responsibility.
Is it blood for oil? I don't know let's wait and see.
We will only know this after the Iraqis are free.
Still our POWs are held and yellow ribbons fly in the
breeze, some are tied around sturdy oak trees.
Sturdy like America in the hopes that our troops
will be home soon.
We pause. After the shock and the awe
we *still* pause.

3/30/03

Whose Child Is This?

Whose child is this who lays to rest upon the ground
is sleeping.
A young man from the states dreams of a better
place where there is no war.
As he takes a quick nap before his duty he dreams
of college and the stories he will tell – when
the war is over and we are free from this hell.
Whose child is this who lays to rest.
A young female soldier passes the ultimate test.
To be in a war fighting alongside her male peers
no earrings in her ears – a woman, yet a soldier
with no fear. Fighting the good fight for democracy.
Fighting the good fight to help others be free.
Whose child is this on the battlefield fighting, refusing
to yield. A faceless child of a divided nation.
Yet fighting to hold onto their location.
Whose child is this…

3/31/03

Opinions

Wherever you go there are those with an opinion to
show.
Some say we don't need to be in that place. Others say
freedom must show her face. Some say war is the only
way.
Others say diplomacy will save the day.
Opinions, opinions, everyone has got one.
Opinions, opinions, but who has the "right" one?
Some people say we are using the wrong strategy.
Others say things are being done perfectly.
Some say our president is a racist hack.
Yet three key characters in this play—are black.
Some say we should have won by now.
Others say this Iraqi field will not be easy to plow.
Our forces have been left with a tough row to hoe.
Yet the opinions just will not cease to flow.
Opinions, opinions, some cruel some kind.
The only ones that matter are in our troops mind.

4/01/03

April's Fool

We thought this war would end soon.
April's fool! April's fool!
We thought our allies could be our tool.
April's fool! April's fool!
We thought diplomacy would work
before we went off to war.
April's fool! April's fool!
We thought all Americans would support the
war. Yet many believe our country is a whore
—for oil.
April's fool! April's fool!
We thought this could be over by now.
We thought with our swords we would now plow.
April's fool! April's fool!
We thought *all* of our POWs would be free
and then we would leave Iraq in democracy.
April's fool! April's fool!
Let's hope with the casualties we have
made the price of peace has been paid.
Our troops need not be used as tools
for they are not anyone's fool.

4/02/03

On The Road To Baghdad

On our merry way. On the road to Baghdad
to kick ass and take names. Little American
flags are planted along our path. The
people will welcome us with a smile or a laugh.
"Well done!" Well done!" They will all say when
Saddam is replaced by the American's stay.
Yes, stay we will in Baghdad until the final
fight. The showdown is drawing to a close,
nowhere to run there will be no flights.
On the road to Baghdad the dust flying
in the air we will liberate the Iraqis and
life will be fair. On the road to
Baghdad democracy is coming, as I hear
the roar of the mechanized units humming.
"Free them!" "Free them!" they seem to say.
The only obstacle is Saddam, we must make
him go away. On the road to Baghdad victory
soon will be ours let us hope our ideals
are real and not amongst the
stars.

4/04/03

"Liberators"

We have been planning this since 1991-92, do they think
the American people are fools.
Leftovers from a previous administration now play
a game of mental masturbation – manipulating an
unsuspecting public.
Telling them this war is for the Iraqi subjects.
If that is so, then why just now. Why didn't we
help when the Kurds and Shiites begged we need
you now. We just turned and walked away, like the
League of Nations with Haile Selassie.
What bastards we are. We have to have gas
to fill up our cars. We Americans get off with
relatively
cheap prices – just ask our brethren in Europe
who find this issue divisive.
Yes, we are the liberators, here we come to
remove terrorism after 911. Afghani, Iraqi,
why me? Caught up in this cynicism
hurling my unwarranted criticism. They say
the troops fighting makes me free.
But that's OK guys, just let me be.

4/05/03

Saturday Night Is A Night For Fighting.

Saturday night is a night for fighting. Away from home
I see the lightning. The shells explode in the distance
with a loud thundering sound. The explosions brighten
the darkness of the night. How much longer will this
thing last as they give a twisted sort of laugh. It is dark
humor that Saddam's political party should be named
Baath, because the coalition forces are showering their
wrath. Downpouring bombs by the hour, giving the
Baath party a "cleansing shower". Who is right and
who is wrong? Is this decided by the weak bowing
down to the strong. Saturday night is a night for
fighting. I see the flashes, much like lightning. I hear
the guns roar and their thunder. I wonder where the
mortars go when there is a blunder. Mothers cry and
children scream, but embedded reporters avoid these
scenes. All we know is that we are number one.
American troops are under the gun. POWs are held but
I hope not forgotten. The sweetness of freedom can
sometimes turn rotten.

Saturday night is a night for a fight. All of Iraq's
wrongs will soon be made "right".

4/6/03

Another Sunday

Another Sunday, time for prayer.
Another Sunday, my child is over there.
Another Sunday, I want this war to end.
Another Sunday, Easter in two weeks begins.
Another Sunday, another holy season,
Another war, another idealistic reason.
Another Sunday will be Palm Sunday. Will
the Iraqis wave flags like the Jews waved palms?
But didn't the Christians blame the Jews for
doing Christ wrong.
Another Sunday, another day,
No chance for peace or to save face.
At this point it is right or wrong.
At this point it is weak against strong.
At this point the war goes on.
Until Johnny or Jane comes marching
home.

4/06/03

Sunday

Sunday should be the day of rest, of quietness yet the war
goes on.
Sunday should be a symbol of reconciliation and resurrection
yet the war goes on.
Sunday should be the day of a visit to your family, a day of
gentleness a day to be free.
Yet the war goes on.
Sunday should be the time of an enjoyable meal with all the
trimmings.
Yet the war goes on.
Sunday should be a day of prayer a day of hope a day in which
we all can cope.
Yet the war goes on.
Yet the world goes on
Yet time goes on.
Yet we go on in our lives, in our trials.
Just another Sunday but this one drives me wild
because our troops are in a loop trying to end this
circular game. Our POWs are *still* being held – what
are their names? Sunday, Sunday can't stand
this day. When will freedom end this fray.

4/07/03

Many Rivers To Cross

"Many Rivers To Cross" the title of a gospel song.
Many Rivers to Cross something right has gone wrong.
A few cameramen were killed today – thought to be
Iraqi snipers
getting in the way. Thousands have died in the
bombings, yet in
the aftermath the streets seem calming. POWs are still
held
and we have not found the big boss; another cross to
bear
—yet many rivers to cross. Many admit winning the
war
should be relatively easy, it is the political control
which
sounds rather sleazy. Who controls what and has a
contract with who sounds like a convoluted story
created
by Dr. Seuss. Here we are with the American stars on
our
belly facing our opponents who don't have any. Must
we
expect them to be like us, to pay for their ticket on the
bus –
of freedom. Here we go again, words are at a loss, so
many more
rivers to cross. Was it blood for oil or blood for
freedom.
The American dream, or pre – Armageddon. No one

263

really knows for sure. All we can do is try not to get lured
by the lies that we are told in the tale of evil and good.
Although some of our troops have had to pay the ultimate cost
we *still*! Yes *still*!
have many rivers to cross.

4/07/03

Inside The City

Inside the city the war goes on.
Inside the city the walls have not fallen.
Inside the city civilians need food.
Inside the city the troops set the mood.
Inside the city we need the lights on.
Inside the city who can we phone.
Inside the city is anyone home.
Inside the city we see the homeless roam.
Inside the city it does not look too pretty.
We now have become aware that war is not fair.
Some die that aren't supposed to. Some live although
you don't want them to. Innocents are injured or
maimed to outlive this war scarred and lame. All of
these faces – I can't remember the names. The POWs
are still being held. Inside the city desperation
is being felt. Inside the city I hear them say as
they run for cover.
    "God/Allah I wish this war was over."

4/08/03

Is He Is Or Is He Ain't.

Once thought dead he could be alive is this truth or is it
jive. Is he is or is he ain't all we can do is wait.
People hope and people pray that those thousands
pounds of bombs have blown him away.
Is he is or is he ain't. We must just sit and wait. The
tyrant seems to have nine lives but we must keep our
hopes alive. We must be sure and endure. Wherever he
is his regime is no more. Is he is or is he ain't. What
ever he could do he no longer can't. The people breath
a heavy sigh as their liberation is nigh. They can't
celebrate just yet. They don't want to get caught in his
net. The net of lies, the net of deception, the net of
propaganda, the feeling of dejection. Is he is or is he
ain't the world holds its breath and waits.

4/09/03

Baghdad Has Fallen
"Babylon the great is fallen…" – (Revelation 18)

The people pull and tug at the statue, sweating from
the strain.
The look of determination and remembrance of the
pain.
The statue gleams defiant and refuses to yield.
Additional marines help the people as others come in
from the field.
Now a small army is pulling and tugging.
The statue topples and there is rejoicing and hugging.
Saddam has fallen statue and all.
"Baghdad has fallen" I hear in a phone call.
"No more Saddam!" "No more Saddam!"
The people thought of as violent are gentle as lambs.
Triumphant, they dance around the fallen figure.
They enter government buildings and haul off
"treasure".
The people seek payment for the years of abuse.
They only take what they can use.
Soldiers stand by, some adorned with flowers; given to
them by Iraqis for enduring these difficult hours.
It will take more than flowers to heal this nation.
All that matters now is gratefulness and elation.
Baghdad has fallen but the war is not over.
The people stand proud not cowering for cover.
The troops have done well, enjoy this day of glory
tomorrow, tomorrow may be another story.

4/10/03

Next Kirkuk?

The fall of Baghdad the approach of Kirkuk,
cities are falling is it skill or just our luck.
Like dominoes they seem to fall. With each one the
civilians call "No Saddam," "No Saddam",
All things seem to be going as planned,
with isolated brush fires waiting to be put out.
The allied forces do not have any doubts.
It does seem that the war is ours.
But it is with the *new* politics that *we*
will see stars. Who must wait and who will
be in charge. Those brought in from exile will
ride in special cars. Some troops will remain
to facilitate the process. Will civilians become
disgruntled about casualties and losses.
Yet the troops stay to fight another day.
Like a loyal dog on a chain, we bring them around
when America must have her way.
Still I wonder why more must die.
I remember the POW's and see their parents
cry. Next I see oil rich Kirkuk.
When it is "liberated" will the Kurds be
forsook, or will there be plans for a rightful
Kurdistan. I guess we have to talk to the
Turks – here we go again.

4/11/03

Sister Soldiers

From Jessica Lynch to Shoshanna Johnson to Lori
Piestewa the sisters in the service are doing their own
thing. Fighting the wars, cutting to the chase my sister
soldiers are all over the place. On land, in the air or
rocking on the sea, our ladies serve with diligence,
power and bravery. Whether behind a desk or in the
field our sisters are fighting refusing to yield. Whether
high in the sky or crawling on the ground our lady
troops are all around.
Showing their love to their big Sister Liberty, these
beautiful flowers have the resolve of a mighty oak tree.
Sister soldiers from all cultures examples to us males;
we know you are not frail. Uncle Sam is not a liar, in
your heart burns the fire:
To aim high; be all that you can be; this is not just a
job it's an adventure. Thanks for your service and
keeping us free. Semper Fi to you and your country.

4/12/03

At The Cradle

At the cradle of civilization it is a clear revelation,
that this place is a troubled nation.
We came to find weapons of mass destruction, yet we have
used weapons to cause destruction among the masses.
And what about the different classes: Shiite, Sunni and
Kurds too. At least three factions who say their way is
truth.
Not to mention others with their own political goals
they are like bandits in the desert digging holes.
Trying to find a lost treasure with what tool do we
use to measure – men's souls.
At the Cradle of Civilization it is now a realization
that a war does not a peace make.
That a regime change does'nt necessarily change
things.
That blood for oil is not a fair sacrifice, especially
when the stakes are our children's lives.
What do we hope to achieve – better yet, what do we
want the people to believe. Standing at my
end of the world looking at the cradle are the
Americans just a workhorse that has been saddled.
To pay for a war and reconstruction of the land
of a people who wish our destruction.
At the cradle the baby cries after being bit
by a snake. "You should have known I was a
snake" he hisses as he slithers away.

4/14/03

The War After The War

Now that we have had the war to set you free who is to
watch you, but me. Government in shambles, looters
roam the streets, national treasures are gone while I
guard the Oil Ministry. Who is to watch you, but me.
Though no weapons of mass destruction have been
found I reason they could have been hid in Syria or
some Iranian town. As far as regime change, well
that's another story. Saddam is now gone but who do
we get to have order at home. What puppet do we
place upon the throne to favor allies oil contracts and
rebuild the Iraqi homes. Have we traded a tyrant for a
sneak. Time will only tell in the upcoming weeks. The
troops have done good hopefully soon they will be
home.
It is a shame chess pieces don't bleed after the game is
done.
The war after the war will definitely be more "fun."
Because – lies told before will have nowhere to run.

4/14/03

Tikrit

Tikrit the city of Saddam.
Hometown of the villain.
Tikrit has fallen uneventfully.
Nonchalant, the people are sullen.
Tikrit the last dot of cities to connect
on a connect the dot odyssey that has stretched
from Basra up to your gates.
Tikrit, Tikrit open the gates the inevitable
will no longer wait.
Hometown of Saddam.
Now you are damned to be the village of
that tyrant who is now vacant or dead.
The people seem sad and are embarrassed instead
of the glowing promise of pride. Former Baath
members have to hide away from
the American victory. Away from the wrath
of the new Iraqis.
Tikrit! Tikrit!
Take heart this is your new start.
You begin your journey new with a
brand new type of shoe. Its called
democracy and its just for you.
Tikrit. Tikrit.
Don't be surprised
You are being fitted for freedom and it *is*
the right size.
The 7 POWs are now freed.
Lord let this be the end.
Let this be the last city.

4/15/03

The End Begins Again

The End begins again, time for this war to end.
The End begins again former exiles are in the country
again.
The End begins again, the old rivalries heat up on the
pot.
The End begins again, potential leaders vie for a spot.
The End begins again, the U.S. is now in charge.
The End begins again, so many challenges, decisions
that
will be hard.
The End begins again, this place is like a zoo.
The End begins again, looting and pillaging reveals
some truths.
The End begins again, others look at our nation with
skepticism
and speculation.
"When will they go for the oil?" The people ask.
"We would never do that." Those in power answer
with a laugh.
The End begins again.
Tomorrow begins new.
I hope we brought the torch of freedom
and not the big screw.

4/16/03

The Party Is Over

The party is over the war is won ships head back home one-by-one. American resolve proves itself again to impose its will on our fellow man. But is this just raw imposition or did much thought go into this mission. True enough we started this war. But Saddam had treated his country much like a whore.

So we were strong and not limp we released Iraq from her former pimp. A pimp we helped keep in power until his own ego brought him to his final hour. Did he not know he could not mess with the U.S. We are the chosen, we are the best.
How dare he think he could compete with US. It just goes to show when you give a little power, a tyrant just wants more. So the party is over. Come on home, the troops will have their stories told many times over the phone and all will glow when they come home. The chess game is over and would you believe that in this case the chess pieces bleed. They are real people like you and me. Let us welcome them back to the land of the "free". Where "democracy" allows the Klan the Skinheads and Neo Nazis. Yes, the party is over and the troops are coming home. Let us practice real freedom and democracy at home.

4/17/03

W.O.M.D.
(Weapons of Mass Destruction)

Time to turn to W.O.M.D. The station where the U.S.
comes to make you free, and spread our love of
democracy, whether Iran, Iraq or North Korea with
station W.O.M.D. things may become more clearer.
Station W.O.M.D. to protect the world, The American
flag is now unfurled.
No need to fret. No need to cry. Just tune into our
station and we will tell you why. We can give you
other nations' capabilities. Maybe it is true or is that
just what we believe. You see with W.O.M.D. we will
make you free, liberate your country—especially if
you have something we need. Tune into W.O.M.D. we
promise to entertain, bring our troops over, drop some
bombs, kick ass and take names. We are W.O.M.D.
and that is what we do. We are supported by tax
dollars and our propaganda too. If you are not good we
will be seeing you – soon.
Station W.O.M.D.
Courtesy of the Red, White and Blue.

4/18/03

We Don't Want You Either

Saddam was a bad man.
But the Americans are not in our plans.
You may have given us a breather.
But we don't want you either.

Saddam abused the people – that is true.
He did more damage – more than you.
The man was a real heathen.
But we don't want you either.

Saddam kept us from being free.
But the freedom that you bring is not really free.
It comes with a price tag and I am not a believer.
You see, we don't want you either.

Saddam has hurt the people for many years.
There has been much bloodshed and untold tears.
Brutality without measure and well known fears.
But our people can take it from here for we *are*
achievers. With thanks and
without malice, we don't want you either.

4/19/03

The Night Before Easter

It was the night before Easter and all through the land
the people all cheered because there was no Saddam.
Children had their baskets in their homes with care in
the hopes that the Easter Bunny soon would be there.
New clothes and new bonnets to end our clothes of
winter. New uniforms and helmets, the future could
not look dimmer. Let's get ready for the parades back
here. When our troops come home they will trade
stories and drink beer. Welcome back from a month
long war. You defeated the enemy even though we
stopped keeping score. No one surrendered officially,
yet.
But if there *is* any resistance we can just send over a
few jets. Drop some bombs in the shape of Easter eggs,
I wonder how many people have lost their legs. For the
most part this war is over. Let us forgive and forget
like long lost lovers we never hold grudges against our
enemies. Just ask the English, French, Spanish,
Italians, Turks, Germans, Russians, Chinese, Japanese,
Vietnamese, Serbians and Somalis. If I left your
country out forgive me please, there is still time for
more wars with my country. As the Easter Bunny
hopped out of sight he said "Happy Easter to all let
there be peace tonight."

4/20/03

Easter

Easter has come, time for the resurrection let us
cling to love instead of destruction.
Hope for this world rises and falls
much like the emotions of a fickle love.
We want power, no one wants to share.
We want resources with prices *we* think are fair.
At Easter we celebrate personal renewel.
Triumph of good over the ultimate evil.
Mystery and forgiveness are the operative words,
of a man's life given for the sins of the world.
It seems so funny how we forget to turn the
other cheek. Knowing if we did we would be
perceived
as weak. I guess for that reason alone would make
Jesus wrong. Yet in his apparent weakness he
was infinitely strong. To abstain from violence when it
is within your grasp is of paramount
importance in a true Christians plans. Yet it surprises
me like never before that such a "Christian" nation
went so easily to war. But I guess there is
no need to worry – God is always on our side.
I wonder if that holds true if we are caught in a lie.
Well enough of this doom and despair pass me
some ham and Happy Easter to those people over
there.

5/1/03

Untie The Yellow Ribbon

Untie the yellow ribbons the troops are coming home
after a month of war in a place not well known. Untie
the yellow ribbons open them up as we open our arms
to embrace the sons and daughters of our country.
Regardless of race, color or creed they were willing to
bleed for our belief that all should live free.
Some paid the ultimate price.
May America never forget their sacrifice. Untie the
yellow ribbon. The color of gold showing the golden
brightness of a country's wealth untold. Yellow also
showing the color of the bellies of politicians and
businessmen who will make untold profits off the
sacrifice of our young like vultures over the freshly
dead, they too wait to see the winds of change, ready to
pounce after the political dust settles.
Untie the yellow ribbon our troops are coming home
without Osama, Saddam or W.O.M.D. (weapons of
mass destruction) – well, at least the Iraqi people are
now free (?)

5/02/03

Love, War And Other White Lies

I love my country and I always will but she reminds
me of a former lover – I will call Jill. Pretty and young
with a smiling face she told little white lies to bolster
my faith. Never realizing I always knew the score but
not wanting to believe she was playing the whore. My
country, my country tis of thee please come back to
sanity, of thee I sing. Land where our children died on
the Iraqi countryside, wanting freedom to ring. The
war is over but not the drama. We still have yet to find
Saddam and Osama not to mention W.O.M.D.
(weapons of mass destruction). Someone tell the North
Koreans they are the next people we will be "freeing."
But wait they already have W.O.M.D., but they don't
have oil – so we may deal with *them* diplomatically.
Can you call democracy, democracy when it is forced.
If you drown a horse making it drink water does it
justify force? Can democracy – real democracy, really
be, if it is forced upon a country? Just as Stalin with
Communism and Hitler with Nazism does it mean a
lack of patriotism if I have criticism. Love, war and
other white lies, don't be surprised if you refuse to
open your eyes.

5/12/03

The Soul Of This Black Folk
(For W.E.B. Du Bois)

One hundred years ago in 1903, you published a book
to hopefully set minds free. Here we sit 100 years later
some pains have lessened while others have become
greater. Though lynchings may be a thing of the past
and I should feel free; a black man in Texas was
dragged by chains from a truck back in the 1990's.
The debate still rings between attaining an occupation
or equal socialization. The struggle continues between
fighting for dignity or grabbing at the first job you see.
The "talented tenth" exists but alas nine tenths of that
tenth have moved up and out. They say class out
weighs race, at least until economic realities hit, then
Black will be Black as it was before. We have come so
far and yet have so far to go, I wish I could pry open
some minds and help modern ideas grow. Yet, some of
us seem bent on living in the past while allowing other
fellow citizens to fall lower in their class. We have
just finished conquering the Iraqi man and we will now
force them undemocratically to be democratic.
Speaking of democracy, Mr. Du Bois we still have
people running around "free" in *our* democracy
wearing white sheets like back in 1903. Though many
have traded their robes for suits they are now more
dangerous than those other coots. You see now *these*
people can change an election and start a war without
remorse or reflection. So since 1903 and the
establishment of the N.A.A.C.P. things have changed

Tony Bethel

yet stayed the same. People still struggle to be "free"
while trying to play the American game.

About the Author

Tony has been writing poetry since the age of ten. This is his third book. His first was "Love is a Butterfly" (1999). His second book was "Before Forty After 9/11" (2002). Tony attended the University of Illinois and received his bachelor's degree in Psychology (1983). He served in the U.S. Navy (1983-93), and was in the Persian Gulf War. In 1998 he graduated Phi Theta Kappa with an A.A.S. from Kankakee Community College. In 1999 he completed his first (and probably last) Chicago Marathon. Tony works with individuals who are developmentally disabled in addition to being a Licensed Massage Therapist and Licensed Physical Therapist Assistant. Tony has three children who are a great source of inspiration. He wrote this book to exercise his right to free speech and expression.